That Patchwork Place®

Appliquilt®

To Go

Tonee White

Dedication

To my "Auntie." She taught me to believe in myself and to know that anything is possible if you dare to make it happen. She is sorely missed.

Acknowledgments

My thanks to:

The wonderful teachers I had early on in my quilting career. Judy Maxwell, Lynn Mann, and Margrit Hall taught me good basics that I build on every day.

All the students who challenge as well as support me in my work.

My husband, Bob, the "saint" who is always there to help and to listen with patience and pride.

Credits

Editor-in-Chief .... Kerry I. Hoffman
Managing Editor .... Judy Petry
Proofreader .... Melissa Riesland
Design Director .... Cheryl Stevenson
Text and Cover Designer .... Amy Shayne
Production Assistant .... Marijane E. Figg
Technical Illustrators .... Brian Metz, Laurel Strand
Illustration Assistant........................... Robin Strobel
Decorative Art .... Barb Tourtillotte
Photographer .... Brent Kane

Appliquilt® to Go
© 1997 by Tonee White
That Patchwork Place, Inc., PO Box 118
Bothell, WA 98041-0118 USA

Printed in the United States of America
02 01 00 99 98 97   6 5 4 3 2 1

The information in this book is presented in good faith, but no warranty is given nor results guaranteed. Since That Patchwork Place, Inc., has no control over choice of materials or procedures, the company assumes no responsibility for the use of this information.

Library of Congress Cataloging -in-Publication Data

White, Tonee,
   Appliquilt to go / Tonee White.
      p. cm.
   ISBN 1-56477-182-2
   1. Appliqué—Patterns. 2. Quilting—Patterns. 3. Patchwork—Patterns.
   I.Title.
   TT779.W5525 1997
   746.46—dc21   96-37093
                                                           CIP

Mission Statement

We are dedicated to providing quality products and service by working together to inspire creativity and to enrich the lives we touch.

Contents

Meet the Author

Tonee White's quilting journey, which began six years ago, has taken her in many exciting and different directions. Within two years of attending her first quiltmaking class, she was designing, teaching, and exhibiting her quilts internationally. A needlepoint and cross-stitch background brought hand skills to her new craft.

Within four years, Tonee joined the world of publishing, first with *Appliquilt: Whimsical One-Step Appliqué and Quilting*, followed by *Appliquilt for Christmas*, and then *Appliquilt Your ABCs*, all published by That Patchwork Place.

Home to Tonee is Irvine, California, where she lives with her husband, Bob, and a few of her seven children. She thoroughly enjoys her four grandchildren, who live close by.

Tonee continues to teach and lecture across the country, and she is currently hard at work on a new book and a new technique.

Introduction

"So many quilts, so little time." Yes, the word has been changed to reflect our passion, but this phrase is true for so many quilters I meet. Greater demands are placed on us every day. Thank heavens we have the conveniences we do. If we had to bake our own bread and churn our own butter along with car pools, soccer practice, and for some, full-time employment, we could never get it all done, let alone find time to quilt.

I can't help feeling that many of us yearn for a slower pace and the serenity that comes with it. We look back with fond memories on the quieter times of our lives. I know I do. This longing for tranquillity has helped to bring about the popularity of the Country look and a renewed interest in quilting.

Not a day goes by that I don't hear someone say, "I'm too busy," but I firmly believe that we can make time for activities that are important to us, even if it's only a few minutes here and there.

The projects in this book are designed to allow you to assemble and stitch each block separately. When the blocks are finished, you join them, attach the borders, and bind the edges. Add your embellishments and you're done!

Working this way, it's easy to tuck a block into a bag and stitch whenever time allows—in the doctor's office, on your lunch hour, on the phone, even while waiting for water to boil. These small pockets of idle time quickly add up to a few hours a week, time enough to make a block or two. Once you try this method, you'll be surprised at how much you can accomplish. As you become more familiar with this method, you'll be able to adapt other patterns and ideas to this technique.

Please use your creativity to make each appliquilt truly yours. Put your address on the house in "Halloween Sampler" (page 23), or appliquilt the family pet onto "Country Sampler" (page 26). I have always considered my designs to be merely suggestions, and I'm always pleased when you redesign them with your personal touch.

Have fun with the process. Remember, time spent stitching is your recreation and reward for hard work. In no time at all, you'll have new additions for your home or wonderful gifts for family and friends.

Choosing Fabric and Supplies

Fabric

Have you noticed what's happened in the fabric industry in the last few years? Quilt shops now burst at the seams with fabrics in every conceivable design and imaginable color. This fabric explosion is the result of the continuing interest in quilting and the ever-increasing number of quilters worldwide.

This huge selection of fabrics is wonderful, but it can also be perplexing. Do choices become easier when the possibilities increase? Not for everyone. For some, it only increases indecisiveness.

Take advantage of this marvelous fabric variety. It's like being given the big box of sixty-four crayons after having been limited to the box of eight. Not only can quilters find fabrics in many colors, but they can also find different scales of prints, stripes, and plaids. Quilters usually have a choice of the type of fabric as well—there are woven homespuns; soft, flowing cottons; stiffer fabrics with a primitive feel; and new, softer flannels that affect the weight as well as the texture of quilts. There are all sorts of amazing fabrics available. What could be more versatile than a fabric that is homespun on one side and flannel on the other? Look upon the fabric revolution as a positive development in quiltmaking. Quilters are like artists, and we are being given lots of new "paint" for our creations.

Fabric choices are important because they affect not only the look but also the weight and texture of the finished quilt. When you appliquilt, you stitch through at least four layers. Softer, more loosely woven fabrics are easiest to work with because they contain less sizing. If you wish to use a stiffer fabric that is not "quilter friendly," wash it in warm water with Orvus® Quilt Soap (which is readily available in quilt shops) and it should soften up nicely.

This brings me to washing fabric. I only wash fabric if it is too stiff to work with comfortably, if the dye rubs off on my hands or sewing machine, or if I wish to tea-dye the fabric. I wash my fabrics and quilts with Orvus Quilt Soap. If a dye runs, Orvus soap holds the dye in suspension and keeps it from invading other fabrics or other areas of the same fabric. For example, if you wash a red-and-white gingham and the red dye bleeds, the water in the washing machine will look red but the dye in the water will not color the white areas of the gingham.

Note

The designs in this book call for many different fabrics. Yardage requirements are given for fabrics you will probably need to purchase for the project, such as the background. For most of the appliqué pieces, scraps are sufficient. If a fabric is not listed, the amount needed is probably 1/8 yard or less.

Tea-Dyeing

With the increased availability of fabrics that appear aged, I am not tea-dying fabric as often as I used to. However, I occasionally need to tone down a fabric that is too bright.

Your fabrics will absorb the tea more readily if you prewash them in Orvus soap to remove the sizing. There is no need to dry the fabrics after washing them, because you're just going to get them wet again.

I use a gallon size, clear glass jar unless I am dyeing a large piece of fabric. A gallon jar allows me to see the fabric and what is happening to the color. I leave the fabric in the dye from one hour to one week. (I never knew tea could grow mold until I became a quilter.)

Recipe for Tea-Dyeing

1 quart hot tap water
3 tablespoons instant coffee
8 tea bags

Stir the instant coffee into the water. Let the tea bags steep in the mixture for a few minutes; remove the bags and soak the prewashed fabric in the dye bath for 20 minutes. Soak longer or even overnight to get darker results. To get a blotchy effect, leave the tea bags in the water with the fabric.

I like to keep a supply of tea-dyed muslin in varying shades. To create a variety of tea-dyed shades, cut five or six fat quarters (18" x 22") of prewashed muslin. Make a double batch of the tea-dyeing recipe, and place the fat quarters in the dye bath. After a couple hours, take out a fat quarter or two. Two or three hours later, take out one or two more fat quarters. The next day, take out another, and so on.

If I am anxious to use a fabric and don't want to wait for the tea-dying process, I spray the piece with tan Rit® dye. I put four to six ounces of dye in a 32-ounce spray bottle and fill it with water. After the fabric is fairly well saturated, spread it on a piece of parchment paper, and place it in a 200°F oven for 30 minutes or until dry. The results are usually blotchy, but the effect is primitive and wonderful.

If, after finishing a quilt, you wish you had tea-dyed the fabric, or if a few fabrics appear too light, you can still tone them down by spraying the quilt with tan Rit dye. Hang your quilt outside and spray it with the dye; then allow the quilt to line dry. I do not rinse the dye out.

Thread

To achieve the primitive look I love, the stitches on an appliquilt should be seen. This characteristic is the single most important criterion in choosing thread. Second is the ease of stitching, and third is color availability.

I use #8 and #12 perle cotton most often. Perle cotton is thick enough to be seen, yet it pulls through the fabric easily because it is tightly twisted. You'll find #8 perle cotton in a wide variety of colors.

Buttonhole twist or top stitching thread is my second choice. Thread of this weight is comfortable to stitch with and comes in a variety of colors. It is nearly interchangeable with #8 or #12 perle cotton.

Three strands of embroidery floss is another possibility. I rarely use floss, but many students begin appliquilting with it because they have it on hand. It is readily available in more than three hundred colors. The disadvantages of floss are that it does not pull through the layers as smoothly as perle cotton, and the strands may separate during stitching.

I also use specialty needlework threads, such as metallics or linen, to achieve a particular look. Be open to trying different threads; you may find one that suits your taste and is comfortable to use.

I can't stress enough how important it is to make your stitching tasks easy and comfortable. You're much more likely to finish projects that you've enjoyed from the start.

Needles and Pins

I choose my needle according to the thread I'm using. For #8 or #12 perle cotton, I prefer a #6 or #7 crewel or embroidery needle. You can use #8 and #9 needles for embroidery floss and lighter-weight threads. The needle length is a matter of personal preference; the needle number refers to the size of the eye.

For stitching with thicker threads, I like Piecemakers® Calico Braided Rug needles. These needles are flattened slightly near the tip, making a larger hole that easily accommodates a thick or rough thread.

To secure the appliqué pieces to the quilt sandwich and baste the layers, I use #2 safety pins. To appliquilt each piece, I secure the edges with two straight pins, one where I begin and another 3" to 4" ahead. As I work my way around the piece, I place one of the pins a few inches ahead of my stitching. This way I don't scratch myself while I stitch. Once I finish appliquilting the piece, I remove the safety pins.

Pinking Shears and Rotary Blades

The ease of Appliquilting lies in the fact that the raw edges of your appliqué pieces are not turned under. You cut out your pieces with pinking shears and stitch them with the raw edges showing. Pinking shears reduce fraying, but they do take a "bite" out of the fabric, which reduces some of the detail. Small, intricate shapes are lost when cut with pinking shears, but this is not usually a problem with my large, simple shapes.

I own almost every type of pinking shear on the market. All are acceptable, but there are differences in the ease with which they work. The configuration of the blade, whether it is the saw-tooth, scallop, or wave, is a matter of taste. I use the wave-blade pinking shear made by Clover® for most of my work. The wave blade takes a little less of a "bite" out of the edge, leaving more detail in the shape. I can use these scissors all day, and often do, and my hand does not tire or get sore.

Beware of the smaller craft scissors that come in a variety of blade designs; they are meant for paper. Some will cut fabric, but they dull quickly.

The newest wave and pinking blades that have their own handle (not the blades that fit on your straight-blade rotary cutter) work well. I use them for larger, straight-sided pattern pieces and straight strips. I have students who use these blades to cut out all their pattern pieces.

I cut no more than two thicknesses of fabric at one time with my cutter, and I press down firmly. It's important to press hard enough when cutting because if the blade skips, it's difficult to go back over the wavy edge.

To protect yourself and the blade, be sure to use the plastic cap. Take great care not to nick the blade because nicks can cause the blade to skip.

When choosing equipment, look for products that are easy and comfortable to use. Remember, if any part of the quiltmaking process is not enjoyable, it is less likely that you will finish your project.

Batting

A quilt made with the Appliquilt to Go method requires batting that maintains smooth, straight edges throughout the stitching process. The precise measurement of the batting is the single most important component in achieving a straight, flat quilt.

Cotton batting distorts easily, which means that after stitching, your pieces will no longer have straight edges. For this reason, I prefer to use Pellon˜ fleece for my quilts because it keeps its shape throughout the block construction. Pellon fleece is not dense (you can see through it), which makes for easy needling and a traditional "thin" look. Because it is somewhat stiff, Pellon fleece is ideal for wall hangings.

When purchasing Pellon fleece, make sure you are getting what you ask for. Students sometimes come to class with Thermolam®, another Pellon product also sold by the yard. Thermolam is much denser, and it tends to stretch. (See "Resources" opposite for batting information.)

My second choice is Warm & Natural™, but the edges of this batting may stretch a bit.

You can try other types of batting if you have scraps you would like to use. I do not, however, recommend it. I have tried other types of battings and was not satisfied with the results.

Embellishments

Embellishments are another way to use your creativity. The buttons, trinkets, ribbon, and lace you add to your quilt make it original and truly yours. If you were fortunate enough to have inherited your grandmother's button box, you no doubt have a vast array of suitable embellishments.

If not, the button industry has provided you with many tempting choices. Porcelain buttons in every conceivable image and color are available at most quilt, fabric, and craft shops. (See "Resources" at right for button sources.)

Craft shops that carry miniatures are also a good source of embellishments. Small baskets of apples, toys, and household items make wonderful decorative details on appliquilts.

Always be on the lookout for embellishments—an active imagination helps. If a trinket or charm is small enough for a quilt and you like it, take it home and add it to your collection. I guarantee you will find a use for it. I have a large drawer filled with goodies, and I add to it continuously. If you keep your eyes open, I'm certain you'll have a healthy stash of embellishments in no time.

Resources

Tools

Clover scissors
For store locations, call 1-800-233-1703

Batting

Pellon fleece
For store locations, call Freudenberg (Pellon)
1-800-408-4536

Embellishments

Ceramic stars, flags, fish, Halloween, hearts, bees, and houses
Apple Creek
3004 Glenfield Lane
Ceres, CA 95307

Small stars on "Halloween Sampler"
DeCuyper
815 La Salle Dr.
Little Rock, AR 72211
1-501-221-3094

Apple pin on "Country Sampler"
(designed by Jeri Baird for Homespun Papers)
Country Loft
8166 La Mesa Blvd.
La Mesa, CA 91941
1-619-466-5411

"Carrots" sign, jelly bean buttons, and wooden pumpkins
Four Bears & Co.
1956 Moreno Ave.
Corona, CA 91719

Rubber Stamps

Stampa Barbara
505 Paseo Nuevo
Santa Barbara, CA 93101

Making the Block Sandwiches

Early in my quilting adventure, I took many classes because I wanted to learn every aspect of the craft. One of the methods I learned, quilt-as-you-go, allows you to quilt each block separately before joining the blocks to make a quilt. I liked the technique because it allowed me to work on small, portable pieces.

There were disadvantages, however, and after learning three different assembly methods, I abandoned the technique. The main objection was the same for each method: stitching the batting together using a standard ¼"-wide seam allowance resulted in bulky seams.

Sometime later I developed the appliquilt method, and as the size of my projects grew, the more cumbersome the stitching became. It was the inconvenience of working on an entire quilt that prompted me to devise a method for appliquilting individual blocks before putting them together—and my method also eliminated the bulky seams.

The Appliquilt to Go method is really very simple: You must start with a batting that will maintain a smooth, straight edge after being cut. If you cut each piece of batting the finished size of the block, you can butt the edges of the batting together and zigzag them for a smooth, non-bulky seam. I also cut the batting and the backing pieces large enough to accommodate the border, eliminating the need for separate pieces.

Each quilt in this book employs this method. I hope you enjoy the Appliquilt to Go technique as much as I have. And I hope this technique creates many more opportunities for you to work on quilt projects. A few minutes here and there add up quickly, and before you know it, you're ready to assemble your blocks into a quilt.

Appliquilt to Go, Step-by-Step

The following detailed directions apply to all the quilts in this book. Read them carefully and refer to them as you cut and assemble your blocks. Special instructions for individual quilts are included in the quilt plans.

Each Appliquilt to Go block has the following components:
- ✔ Backing fabric
- ✔ Batting
- ✔ Background fabric
- ✔ Appliqué pieces
- ✔ Embellishments

As in all appliquilt projects, you begin by assembling a quilt sandwich. This sandwich consists of the backing fabric, the batting, and the background fabric. (Do not confuse the backing and background fabrics. The backing is the fabric on the back of the quilt; the background is the foundation fabric for the appliqué pieces.) In the Appliquilt to Go method, each block is a separate sandwich.

The dimensions of the three pieces differ, depending on the location of the block in the quilt. Blocks can be identified as either corner, middle, or center.

Border		
Corner block	Middle block	Corner block
Middle block	Center block	Middle block
Corner block	Middle block	Corner block

Let's take a look at the batting, backing, and background for each of the three blocks. We'll start with the batting because it's easiest to understand.

Batting

Cut the batting piece for the center block (or other blocks that do not touch the border) the finished size of the block, without a seam allowance. Because the batting pieces are butted together and zigzagged, there is no need for a seam allowance.

For blocks that touch the border, cut the batting the finished size of the block, plus the finished width of the border. Again, do not include seam allowances. Using a 12" block and a 2" border as an example, here are the dimensions for the batting pieces used in the three types of blocks:

    Center block: 12" x 12" batting
    Corner block: 14" x 14" batting
    Middle block: 14" x 12" batting

```
┌──────────────────────────────────┐
│          2" Border                │
│  ┌──────────┬──────────┬────────┐ │
│  │14" x 14" │          │        │ │
│  │ Corner   │          │        │ │
│  ├──────────┼──────────┼────────┤ │
│  │14" x 12" │12" x 12" │        │ │
│  │ Middle   │ Center   │        │ │
│  ├──────────┼──────────┼────────┤ │
│  │          │          │        │ │
│  └──────────┴──────────┴────────┘ │
└──────────────────────────────────┘
```

Backing

Backing pieces must include seam allowances, which you turn under on the back of the quilt. On edges that touch other blocks, I **use a ½"-wide seam allowance** because it gives me more to work with.

On edges that include the border, add the finished width of the border, but do not include a seam allowance. Here are the dimensions of the backings used in the three types of blocks:

    Center block: 13" x 13" backing
    Corner block: 14½" x 14½" backing
    Middle block: 14½" x 13" backing

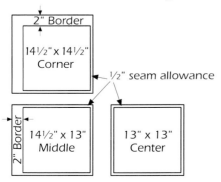

Background

You'll also need to include seam allowances on the background pieces. On edges that touch other blocks, **use a ½"-wide seam allowance**. On edges that touch the border, **add a ¼"-wide seam allowance.** Here are the dimensions of the backgrounds used in the three types of blocks:

    Center block: 13" x 13" background
    Corner block: 12¾" x 12¾" background
    Middle block: 12¾" x 13" background

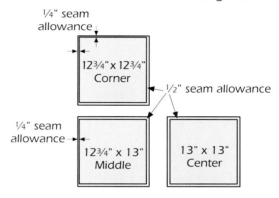

Tip

To help you remember which seam allowance is ½" and which is ¼", visualize the block. On the edges that will be joined to other blocks, the seam allowance is ½". On edges that will be joined to the border, it is ¼".

Cut all of your backings, battings, and backgrounds as directed in the quilt plan, and layer each sandwich according to the following instructions. The examples are based on a 12" x 12" block and a 2"-wide border.

Corner Blocks

The corner blocks have exposed batting on two sides for the borders. The dimensions of the pieces in a 12" corner block that touches a 2" border are:

    14½" x 14½" backing
    14" x 14" batting
    12¾" x 12¾" background

To assemble a corner-block sandwich:

1. Place a backing piece, right side down, on a flat surface. Place the batting for this block on top of the backing. Align the edge of the batting with the edge of the backing on what will be the outer edge of the finished quilt. On the remaining two edges, a ½" backing seam allowance will extend beyond the batting.

2. Place the background, right side up, on top of the block sandwich. Align the ½"-wide seam allowance edges of the background and backing; leave the batting exposed for the border.

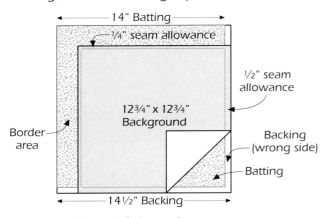

14" Batting
¼" seam allowance
½" seam allowance
12¾" x 12¾" Background
Border area
Backing (wrong side)
Batting
14½" Backing

Upper Left Corner Square

Middle Blocks

A middle block is rectangular, with exposed batting on the border edge and seam allowances on the remaining three edges. The dimensions of the pieces in a 12" middle block that touches a 2" border are:

14½" x 13" backing
14" x 12" batting
12¾" x 13" background

To assemble a middle-block sandwich:

1. Place a backing piece, right side down, on a flat surface. Place the batting for this block on top of the backing, aligning the edges of one short side. On the remaining three edges, a ½"-wide backing seam allowance will extend beyond the batting.
2. Place the background, right side up, on top of the batting, aligning the seam allowances on three sides and leaving the batting exposed for the border.

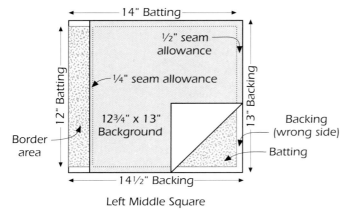

14" Batting
½" seam allowance
¼" seam allowance
12" Batting
13" Backing
12¾" x 13" Background
Border area
Backing (wrong side)
Batting
14½" Backing

Left Middle Square

Center Block

The center block is the only one that does not have an adjoining border, so it has no exposed batting. The dimensions of the pieces in a 12" center block example are:

13" x 13" backing
12" x 12" batting
13" x 13" background

To assemble a center-block sandwich:

1. Place a backing piece, right side down, on a flat surface. Center the batting on the backing, leaving a ½"-wide backing seam allowance all around.
2. Place the background, right side up, on top of the batting, aligning the edges of the backing and the background.

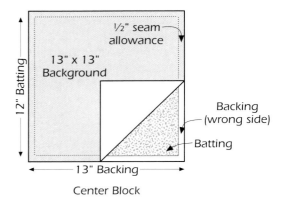

½" seam allowance
12" Batting
13" x 13" Background
Backing (wrong side)
Batting
13" Backing

Center Block

After layering all the block sandwiches, pin them carefully with safety pins to avoid shifting.

Arrange the blocks on a table or on the floor in the quilt configuration. Check to see that you have the proper seam allowances on each block and exposed batting around the entire perimeter of your quilt. Correct any errors now, before you begin to stitch.

Cutting Out the Appliqué Pieces

You need to make templates from the pattern pieces provided for each quilt plan. I prefer the slightly opaque template plastic that comes in flat sheets. It's easy to see through, and it lies flat, providing a firm edge for accurate tracing. Some template plastic sheets come rolled and they seem to want to stay that way; it's a continuous fight to keep the sheet flat while you trace and cut.

You can, of course, use paper to make templates, but paper doesn't provide a firm edge for tracing; it distorts and tears much more easily than plastic.

1. Trace your pattern shapes onto the template plastic using a #2 pencil. Cut out the templates on the traced line with paper scissors.

2. To make the design exactly as it is pictured on the page, place the templates right side down on the wrong side of the fabric. I use a #2 pencil to trace designs on light- and medium-colored fabrics and a white or pastel chalk-type pencil for dark fabrics.

3. Using your pinking shears or pinking blade, cut out the appliqué pieces on the traced line (no seam allowances here).

4. Place and pin each piece on the appropriate quilt sandwich. Pay careful attention to the edges of the batting as you position the pieces. You need at least 1/4" between the appliquilting and the edge of the batting for assembly. If you wish to place an appliqué piece closer to the edge, stitch the piece after you join the blocks.

Tip
Label each quilt sandwich by pinning one prominent, identifiable appliqué piece to the appropriate block.

Learning to Appliquilt

It is the stitching that gives an appliquilt its charm, and happily, it is easy to do. Begin stitching on top of the block, leaving a 4"- to 6"-long tail. Using a simple running stitch, sew through all layers, attaching your appliqué piece to the sandwich and quilting the block at the same time. Stitch a scant ¼" from the edge of the appliqué piece.

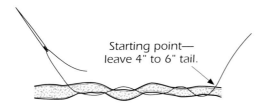

Starting point—
leave 4" to 6" tail.

Don't worry about the size or uniformity of your stitches. The larger and more uneven or crooked they are, the more primitive your work will look. Strive for perfection if that's your style, but remember that perfection is not required.

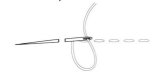

Running Stitch

Continue stitching around the entire piece. When you return to where you began, end the stitching on the top and tie the two threads together in a square knot (right over left and left over right). Clip the ends, leaving a ¼"-long tail. The knot sits proudly on top and adds to the primitive look.

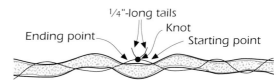

¼"-long tails

Ending point   Knot

Starting point

Knot and trim to ¼"-long tails.

If you run out of perle cotton before you finish stitching a piece, leave a tail at that point. Thread up and begin stitching where you ended, again leaving a tail. Take a few stitches, and then tie the two tails in a square knot.

That's how quick and easy appliquilting is. You appliqué each piece to the block and quilt it in one step, without worrying about turning under seam allowances, appliquéing smooth curves, or making tiny, invisible stitches. Enjoy!

After all the blocks have been stitched, you are ready to join them. I do not add embellishments until all the stitching is complete. Some embellishments may be large or hang from the surface, and these can get in the way or distort the block due to their weight.

Lay the blocks on a flat surface and check to see that the edges line up and that the proper amount of batting shows on the border edges of the corner and middle blocks. Also check to see that you have adequate seam allowances.

1. Working with two side-by-side blocks, such as a middle block and the center block, turn back the seam allowances on both the backing and background pieces to expose the batting at least ½" or more; pin.

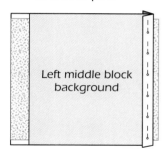

2. Butt the edges of the batting and, using a wide zigzag stitch, join the blocks. Be careful not to overlap the batting; overlapping edges cause lumpy seams and uneven blocks. Join all the blocks in a row or section.

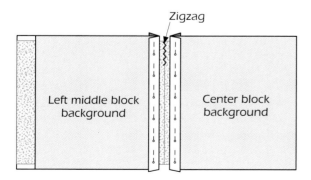

3. Place the row or section right side down on a flat surface. Smooth one backing seam allowance over the zigzagged seam; smooth the other seam allowance over the first. Turn under the raw edge on the top seam allowance and pin.

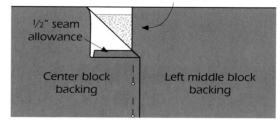

Back of Quilt

4. Using a single thread, blindstitch the folded edge to the backing. Be careful not to catch the batting as you stitch.

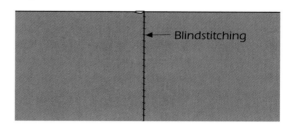

Back of Quilt

5. Join the remaining blocks into rows or sections in the same manner. Join the rows or sections.

6. Lay the quilt right side up on a flat surface. Smooth the backgrounds and turn under the seam allowances as you did on the back of the quilt, adjusting the seams so the corners meet. Pin the seam allowances in place.

7. Using perle cotton or other thread, stitch the seams together. I used a cross stitch or fly stitch on all the projects except "Baskets, Etc." I appliquéd leaves on the seams of this quilt.

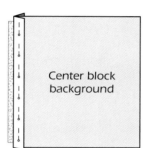

Front of Quilt

Fly Stitch

1. Knot your thread. Come up with your needle from the back of the quilt ¼" to the left of the folded edge of the seam (A). Go down ¼" to the right of the folded edge (B), but do not pull the thread tight. Come up on the folded edge, ½" ahead of the first two points (C), catching the loop of thread.

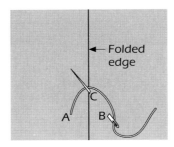

2. Go down next to the emerging thread, tacking the loop in place.

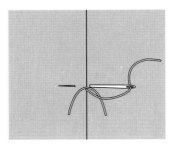

3. Come up ¼" to left of the folded edge, parallel to the tack stitch (D). Go down ¼" to the right of the folded edge (E) and come up ½" ahead (F), again catching the loop. Repeat for a line of stitches.

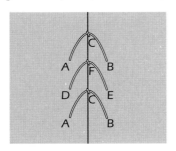

Cross Stitch

1. Knot your thread. Come up with your needle from the back of the quilt ¼" from the folded edge of the seam (A). Go down ¼" from the folded edge on the opposite side of the seam and up ½" (B). Come up on opposite side of the seam (C), parallel to B.

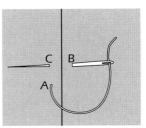

2. Go down ½" below B, crossing over the thread to complete the cross stitch. Come up at E to start the next stitch.

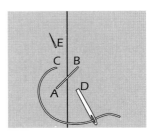

If you prefer, finish the seams with a decorative machine stitch. Another option is to appliquilt shapes over the seams using a blindstitch and matching thread. See "Baskets, Etc." on page 26. Using a decorative stitch or motif for the seams is another opportunity for you to display your creativity.

Adding the Borders

Once the blocks are joined, you're ready to add the borders. The directions for each quilt plan include the dimensions for the borders and the sewing order.

Note

I use ¼"-wide seam allowances to stitch the borders to the quilt top. To allow for the take-up that occurs when you stitch and flip the borders, I cut each border an extra ¼" wide. For a 2"-wide finished border (the border width for the quilts in this book), I cut my strips 2½" wide. After you attach the strips and flip them right side up, you may need to trim them flush with the batting.

1. Place the first border or borders on top of the blocks, right side down and raw edges aligned. Pin in place. Using a ¼"-wide seam allowance, machine stitch through all layers.

Batting
Wrong side of border strip
¼" seam allowance
Left middle block

2. Flip the borders right side up, covering the exposed batting; press the seams.
3. Attach the remaining borders in the same way, covering the ends of the first two borders.

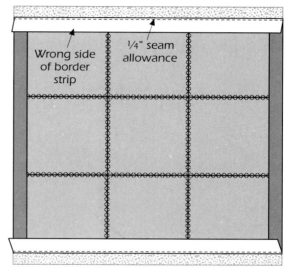

Wrong side of border strip
¼" seam allowance

Binding the Edges

Any binding method is suitable for appliquilts, so if you have a favorite, by all means use it. I have used both a traditional folded binding and an appliquilt binding on the quilts in this book. Following is the appliquilt method:

1. Cut 1¼"- to 1½"-wide binding strips using your pinking shears or blade. Fold the strips in half lengthwise, wrong sides together; press.
2. Trim the batting and backing to match the quilt top. Wrap the binding strip around the raw edge of the quilt, matching the fold with the edge.

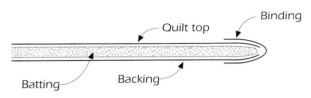

3. Pin at the beginning and 6" from the first pin.

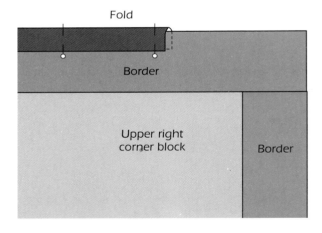

4. Start stitching approximately 1" from the end of the binding strip. Using perle cotton or other thread and the same running stitch you used for appliquilting, stitch ¼" from the pinked edge of the binding, through all layers. Continue stitching, pinning the binding to the quilt approximately 12" ahead of your stitching. (Pinning just 12" ahead prevents scratches and pin pricks.)

   When you need to add another binding strip, simply overlap the ends of the strips 1", take 2 stitches where the strips overlap, then continue. This eliminates the need to sew binding strips together before you begin.
5. Miter the corners as you approach them by folding and pinning. I take two stitches in the corners to secure the folds. Check the back of the quilt to make sure you catch the fold of the miter on the back as well as on the front.

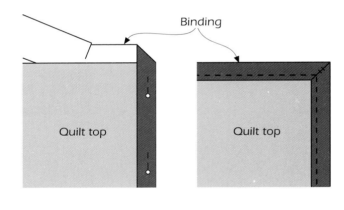

Adding Embellishments

"Save the best for last." I always add my embellishments at the end, after the blocks have been joined and the stitching is complete. For me, embellishments are the "frosting" on my quilts and are what really make them interesting. Embellishments are a most inventive design tool.

Adding embellishments at the end of your project is practical as well. If you attach a dimensional or hanging embellishment to a block in progress, it can distort the block and get in the way when you join the blocks, causing uneven seams. Embellishment instructions are given with some of the block instructions, but always consider the size and the weight of the object.

Buttons

To attach buttons to your quilt, use perle cotton or embroidery floss.

1. Position the button on the quilt. Beginning on the top of the button, stitch through the button and all the layers, leaving a 4"- to 6"-long tail.
2. Stitch through the button holes at least once, ending with the thread on top, opposite the starting tail. Tie a square knot and clip the ends to ⅛" to ¼".

To add embellishments that do not have holes or loops, cut a length of perle cotton, topstitching thread, or other heavy thread 8" long. Attach the midpoint of the thread to the back of the object with an epoxy-type glue, following the instructions on the tube.

When the glue is dry, thread the two ends, one at a time, and stitch the embellishment to your quilt. Tie the ends together on the back. If the object is large or heavy, you may want to glue two or three pieces of thread to the back of it to attach it more securely.

Lace and Ribbon

Attach bits of lace or ribbon by sewing a button here and there. The way in which you attach embellishments can be as creative as the embellishments themselves.

Yo-Yos

Almost any circular motif can be created using yo-yos. Yo-yos add dimension and texture, which can enhance your design. Here's how to make them the quick-and-easy appliquilt way.

1. Use your pinking shears or pinking blade to cut a circle. A finished yo-yo will be approximately half the size of the cut circle.
2. Thread a needle with perle cotton and tie a knot 6" from the end of the thread. With the right side of the fabric facing you, stitch around the circle ⅛" to ¼" from the edge using a running stitch, gathering the fabric against the knot as you go.
3. When you have stitched around the entire circle, turn it over so that the gathers are facing up. Place your index finger in the center hole and adjust the gathers around it.
4. Flatten the yo-yo so that the hole is in the center of the circle. With the thread still in the needle, tie a square knot using the tail you left when you began. Do not take the thread out of the needle.

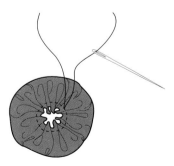

5. Attach the yo-yo to the quilt, placing a button on top if desired. Pull the tails through the button holes. Take a stitch over the hole and tie the tails in a knot; trim. For some flowers, I run the needle through the yo-yo at the folded edge, and then stitch the edge to the quilt or to another yo-yo.

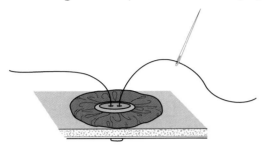

Three-Dimensional Motifs

Another way to add texture to a quilt is to make an object three-dimensional. Follow the directions for "Flowers" to make ears, eggs, and a basket for "Easter Sampler" (page 25).

Flowers

See "Baskets, Etc." on page 26 for examples of three-dimensional flowers.
1. Fuse a piece of Pellon Fusible Fleece to a piece of muslin slightly larger than your pattern piece. With the right side of your flower fabric facing up, trace around the template.
2. Pin the flower fabric to the fleece and appliquilt on the marked line through all layers. Using pinking shears or a pinking blade, cut out the piece ⅛" to ¼" beyond the stitching.
3. Attach the flowers to your quilt with buttons, or tack them with knots.

Buds

See "Baskets, Etc." on page 26 for examples of three-dimensional buds.
1. Make a small yo-yo as explained on page 19. Gather and flatten the circle so that the pinked edges meet and the hole is small.

2. Bring your threaded needle to the ungathered side of the yo-yo and draw the thread up through the middle; pull the thread tight.

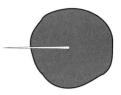

3. Repeat twice, spacing the thread evenly around the yo-yo to form 3 petals. Attach the bud to block with the gathered side down, tying off the threads on the back.

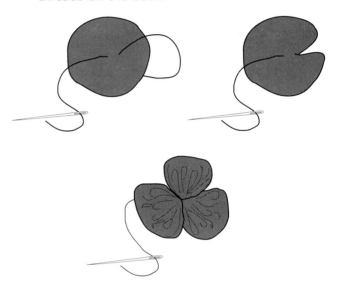

Embroidery

I embroider my appliquilt blocks using embroidery floss. It's softer and more pliable than perle cotton or buttonhole twist, and it lies flat on the fabric. The two stitches I use most often are the backstitch and the French knot.

Backstitch

French Knot

The Appliquilts

"Nantucket" by Tonee White, 1996, Irvine, California, 32" x 26".
A towering lighthouse and seashore motifs capture the feeling of the sea.
Directions begin on page 88.

"Americana" by Tonee White, 1995, Irvine, California, 40" x 25". A trio of flags, a proud eagle, and a soaring angel evoke our patriotic spirit in this folk-art wall hanging.
Directions begin on page 94.

"Apple Sampler"
by Tonee White, 1994,
Irvine, California, 28" x 28".
Classic blocks and apple fixins'
add to the appeal of this bright
wall hanging. Directions begin
on page 43.

"Pumpkin Sampler"
by Tonee White, 1994,
Irvine, California, 28" x 28".
Traditional blocks adorn this
pumpkin-patch wall quilt. Rich
colors convey the feeling of fall.
Directions begin on page 48.

"Halloween Sampler"
by Tonee White, 1994,
Irvine, California,
24" x 28".
Familiar characters
make for a wall quilt
that scares no one but
delights all. Directions
begin on page 84.

"Halloween Quilt"
by Donna Kuehl, 1996,
Rochester, Indiana,
24" x 28".

"Baltimore Album"
by Tonee White, 1995,
Irvine, California, 34" x 34".
A swag-and-bow border frames
classic Baltimore Album designs.
Directions begin on page 62.

"Traditional Sampler"
by Tonee White, 1993,
Irvine, California, 40" x 40".
Traditional motifs set a homey
mood. A scrap border sur-
rounds the blocks and unifies
the design. Directions begin
on page 37.

"Easter Sampler"
by Tonee White, 1993,
Irvine, California, 40" x 40".
Everything that makes Easter
special can be found in this bright,
happy wall quilt. Directions begin
on page 50.

"Carrot Stew"
by Sandie Rayburn, 1995,
Chula Vista, California,
40" x 40".

"Baskets, Etc."
by Tonee White, 1995,
Irvine, California, 44" x 44".
Baskets overflow with
three-dimensional flowers
in this appliquilt tribute to
the garden. Directions
begin on page 68.

"Country Sampler"
by Tonee White, 1994,
Irvine, California, 22" x 22".
Favorite country colors and motifs
combine for a cozy wall quilt.
Directions begin on page 33.

"A Country Sampling"
by Tonee White, 1995,
Irvine, California, 40" x 52".
A scrappy plaid border surrounds
twelve familiar country vignettes.
Directions begin on page 55.

"California Primitive"
by Myrna Kanning Bianchi, 1995,
Irvine, California, 40" x 52".

"Christmas Sampler"
by Tonee White, 1994,
Irvine, California, 22" x 22".
Holiday motifs nestled among
Log Cabin blocks say "Merry
Christmas!" Directions begin
on the facing page.

"Appliquilt Christmas Fun"
by Arvada Trickle, 1995,
Laketon, Indiana, 22" x 22".

Christmas Sampler

A patchwork Santa and tree, Log Cabin blocks, and a gingerbread house bring primitive style home for the holidays.

Color photo: page 28
Size: 22" x 22"
Materials: 44"-wide fabric

¼ yd. each of green, red, and blue prints for block backgrounds

½ yd. Pellon fleece or other thin batting

⅝ yd. fabric for backing

Scraps

    Assorted reds for Log Cabin blocks, Santa, wreath, cottage, and stocking

    Assorted greens for Log Cabin blocks, yo-yos, and tree

    Assorted browns for Log Cabin blocks, cottage, and tree

¼ yd. fabric for border

¼ yd. fabric for binding

Perle cotton in off-white and brown

1 yd. thick wool yarn for Santa beard

Raffia for wreath bow

Buttons of your choice

Embellishments of your choice, such as miniature Santa and bells

Cutting

From the background fabrics, cut:
    1 square, 7" x 7", for center block
    4 rectangles, each 6¾" x 7", for middle blocks

From the batting, cut:
    1 square, 6" x 6", for center block
    4 rectangles, each 6" x 8", for middle blocks
    4 squares, each 8" x 8", for corner blocks

From the backing fabric, cut:
    1 square, 7" x 7", for center block
    4 rectangles, each 7" x 8½", for middle blocks
    4 squares, each 8½" x 8½", for corner blocks

From the assorted reds, cut:
    4 squares, each 2" x 2", for Log Cabin blocks
    6 rectangles, each 2¼" x 3", for Santa

From the assorted greens and browns, cut:
    1¼"-wide strips for Log Cabin blocks
    6 rectangles, each 2" x 2½", for tree

From the border fabric, cut:
    2 strips, each 2½" x 18½", for side borders
    2 strips, each 2½" x 22", for top and bottom borders

Making the Log Cabin Blocks

Using the 2" red squares and 1¼"-wide green and brown strips, make 4 Log Cabin blocks. Quilt the blocks as desired.

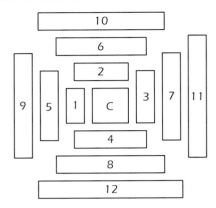

Making the Block Sandwiches

Refer to the instructions on pages 10–12 to layer and label the block sandwiches.

Appliquilting the Blocks

Use the templates on pages 31–32. Refer to the quilt plan for layout of the pieces. The numbers on the templates indicate the stitching order.

1. Make the templates and cut out the appliqué pieces, referring to the instructions on page 13.
2. Appliquilt the pieces, referring to the instructions on page 14. Special instructions for specific blocks follow.

Block #1	Block #2	Block #3
Block #4	Block #5	Block #6
Block #7	Block #8	Block #9

Block Layout Diagram

Block #2: Santa

1. Sew the red rectangles together into 2 rows of 3 pieces each, using ¼"-wide seam allowances.
2. Place the Santa template diagonally on the pieced unit; trace and cut out with pinking shears.

3. Appliquilt the Santa. Cross-stitch (page 16) some of the seams.
4. For the beard, make loops of the wool yarn, approximately 4" long, ending with 2 short loops for the mustache. Stitch to Santa's face.

Block #4: Wreath

Make 8 green yo-yos (page 19) and sew them to the block with buttons. For the bow, tear a 1" x 14" strip of red fabric. Tie the strip in a bow. Tie two 20" pieces of raffia in a bow. Place the fabric bow and the raffia bow on top of the wreath. Attach with a button.

Block #5: House

Cut the snow pieces from thin batting. Cut a motif from printed fabric for the window over the door.

Block #6: Tree

Sew the green and brown rectangles together into 2 rows of 3 pieces each. Place the tree template on the pieced unit; trace and cut out with pinking shears. Appliquilt the tree, catching the trunk in the stitching. Cross-stitch (page 00) the seams.

Block #8: Stocking

1. Stitch the stocking, right sides together, using a ¼"-wide seam allowance. Turn and press.
2. Stitch the heel and toe pieces to the stocking, stitching through the top layer only.
3. Working from the back, tack the stocking to the block in three or four places, catching only the underside of the stocking.

Assembling and Finishing the Quilt

1. Arrange the blocks as shown in the block layout and quilt plan. Join the blocks into rows; join the rows (page 15).
2. Cross-stitch (page 16) the seams if desired.
3. Add the side borders; add the top and bottom borders (page 17).
4. Bind the edges using your favorite method or the appliquilt method (page 18).
5. Attach buttons as desired. Label your quilt.

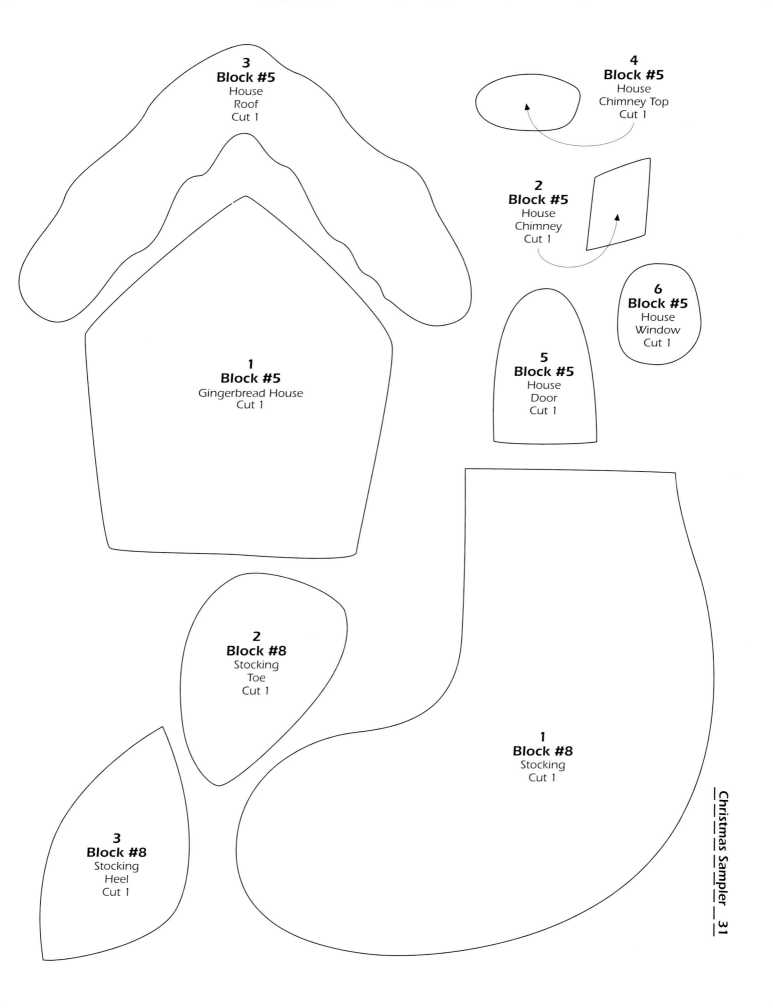

3
Block #5
House
Roof
Cut 1

4
Block #5
House
Chimney Top
Cut 1

2
Block #5
House
Chimney
Cut 1

6
Block #5
House
Window
Cut 1

1
Block #5
Gingerbread House
Cut 1

5
Block #5
House
Door
Cut 1

2
Block #8
Stocking
Toe
Cut 1

1
Block #8
Stocking
Cut 1

3
Block #8
Stocking
Heel
Cut 1

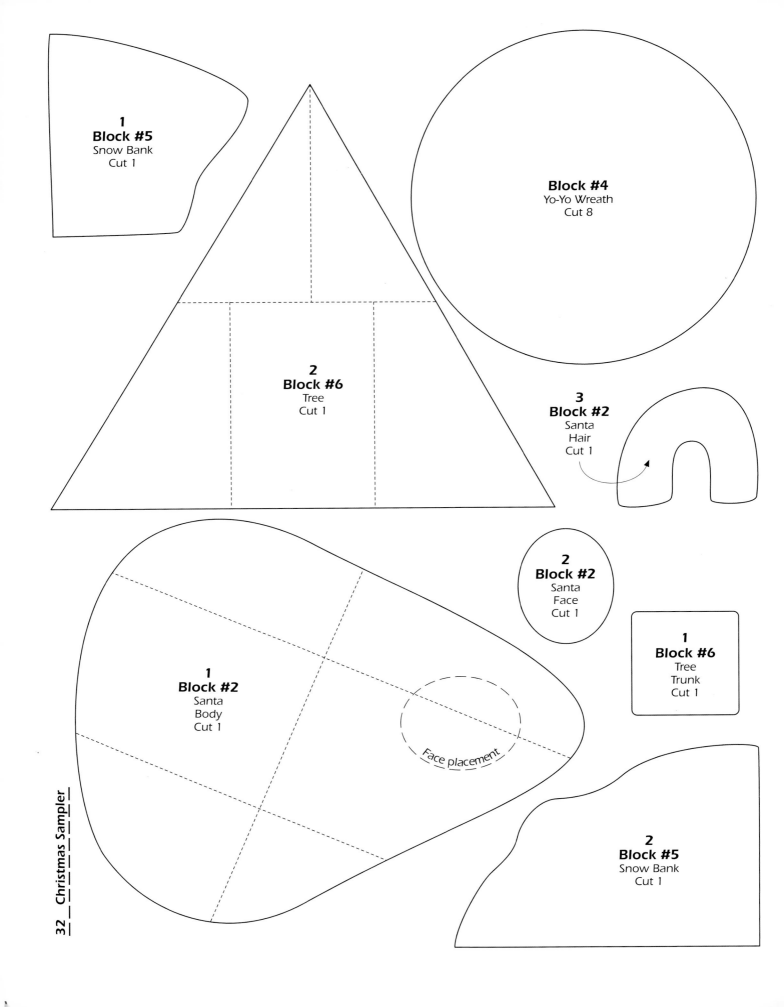

1
Block #5
Snow Bank
Cut 1

2
Block #6
Tree
Cut 1

Block #4
Yo-Yo Wreath
Cut 8

3
Block #2
Santa
Hair
Cut 1

2
Block #2
Santa
Face
Cut 1

1
Block #6
Tree
Trunk
Cut 1

1
Block #2
Santa
Body
Cut 1

Face placement

2
Block #5
Snow Bank
Cut 1

Country Sampler

Strawberries, flowers, bees, and a birdhouse are a few of the things included in this Country collection. What a great gift to make in a hurry for a friend or for yourself.

Color photo: page 26
Size: 22" x 22"
Materials: 44"-wide fabric

¼ yd. muslin for center- and corner-block backgrounds

¼ yd. pink stripe for middle-block backgrounds

½ yd. Pellon fleece or other thin batting

⅝ yd. fabric for backing

¼ yd. fabric for border

Assorted scraps for appliqué pieces

¼ yd. fabric for binding

Black perle cotton

Raffia for wreath

Buttons of your choice, such as bees, bird, pig, flag, stars, and heart

Embellishments of your choice, such as ribbon, lace, apple pin, and heart and hand charms

Cutting

From the muslin, cut:
    1 square, 7" x 7", for center block
    4 squares, each 6¾" x 6¾", for corner blocks

From the pink stripe, cut
    4 rectangles, each 6¾" x 7", for middle blocks

From the batting, cut:
    1 square, 6" x 6", for center block
    4 rectangles, each 6" x 8", for middle blocks
    4 squares, each 8" x 8", for corner blocks

From the backing fabric, cut:
    1 square, 7" x 7", for center block
    4 rectangles, each 7" x 8½", for middle blocks
    4 squares, each 8½" x 8½", for corner blocks

From the border fabric, cut:
    2 strips, each 2½" x 18½", for side borders
    2 strips, each 2½" x 22", for top and bottom borders

Making the Block Sandwiches

Refer to the instructions on pages 10–12 to layer and label the block sandwiches.

Appliquilting the Blocks

Use the templates on pages 35–36. Refer to the quilt plan for layout of the pieces. The numbers on the templates indicate the stitching order.

1. Make the templates and cut out the appliqué pieces, referring to the instructions on page 13.
2. Appliquilt the pieces, referring to the instructions on page 14. Special instructions for specific blocks follow.

Block #1	Block #2	Block #3
Block #4	Block #5	Block #6
Block #7	Block #8	Block #9

Block Layout Diagram

Block #1: Apple

Appliquilt the apple and the stem. Attach the leaf with a button.

Block #2: Wreath

Tear 4 pieces of fabric, each ¾" x 6". Wind two 36"- to 40"-long strands of raffia to form a circle approximately 5" in diameter. Tie the wreath with the strips, spacing them evenly. Attach the wreath to the block by sewing a button (page 20) through the knot on each strip and into the block.

Block #3: Birdhouse

Appliquilt the birdhouse and the branch to the block. Fuse 2 scraps of green fabric. Trace the small leaf pattern and cut out the leaves with straight scissors. Attach each leaf to the block with a small knot in the corner.

Block #5: Bee Hive

Using 3 strands of black perle cotton, backstitch (page 20) curved lines for the bees.

Block #6: Hand

Appliquilt the hand to the block, placing a small piece of lace under the wrist if you like. Sew a narrow satin ribbon to the center of the hand and tie on the heart charm.

Block #7: Flowers

Appliquilt the flower pot to the block. Make 3 yo-yos (page 19) and sew them to the flower pot with buttons.

Block #9: Flag

1. Cut 2 strips of red fabric, each 1¼" x 3", and 1 strip of white fabric, 1¼" x 3". Sew the strips together with the white strip in the middle.
2. Cut a 2¾" x 3¼" navy blue rectangle. Sew the navy blue rectangle to the short edge of the strip unit using a ¼"-wide seam allowance.
3. Cut 1 strip each of red and white fabric, 1¼" x 5½". Sew the strips together. Sew this unit to the lower edge of the first unit.

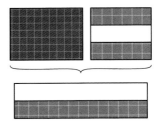

4. Pink the edges of the flag.

Assembling and Finishing the Quilt

1. Arrange the blocks as shown in the block layout and quilt plan. Join the blocks into rows; join the rows (page 15).
2. Fly-stitch (page 16) the seams if desired.
3. Add the side borders; add the top and bottom borders (page 17).
4. Bind the edges using your favorite method or the appliquilt method (page 18).
5. Attach buttons as desired. Label your quilt.

Block #6
Hand
Cut 1

4
Block #3
Leaf
Cut 3

2
Block #3
Birdhouse
Roof
Cut 1

Block #4
Pig
Cut 1

1
Block #3
Birdhouse
Cut 1

3
Block #3
Branch
Cut 1

1
Block #1
Apple
Cut 1

3
Block #1
Apple
Leaf
Cut 1

2
Block #1
Apple
Stem
Cut 1

Block #5
Bee Hive
Cut 1

1
Block #8
Strawberry
Cut 3

2
Block #8
Strawberry
Stem
Cut 3

Traditional Sampler

These traditional blocks are easy to make the appliquilt way.

Color photo: page 24
Size: 40" x 40"
Materials: 44"-wide fabric

1 ⅛ yds. homespun for background

1 ⅓ yds. Pellon fleece or other thin batting

1 ¾ yds. fabric for backing

¼ yd. each of 4 colored prints for appliqué
    pieces and pieced border

¼ yd. fabric for binding

Black perle cotton

Buttons of your choice

Cutting

From the homespun, cut:
    1 square, 13" x 13", for center block
    4 rectangles, each 12¾" x 13", for middle blocks
    4 squares, each 12¾" x 12¾", for corner blocks

From the batting, cut:
    1 square, 12" x 12", for center block
    4 rectangles, each 12" x 14", for middle blocks
    4 squares, each 14" x 14", for corner blocks

From the backing fabric, cut:
    1 square, 13" x 13", for center block
    4 rectangles, each 13" x 14½", for middle blocks
    4 squares, each 14½" x 14½", for corner blocks

Making the Block Sandwiches

Refer to the instructions on pages 10–12 to layer and label the block sandwiches.

Appliquilting the Blocks

Use the templates on pages 39–42. Refer to the quilt plan for layout of the pieces. The numbers on the templates indicate the stitching order.

1. Make the templates and cut out the appliqué pieces, referring to the instructions on page 13.
2. Appliquilt the pieces, referring to the instructions on page 14.

Block #1	Block #2	Block #3
Block #4	Block #5	Block #6
Block #7	Block #8	Block #9

Block Layout Diagram

Assembling and Finishing the Quilt

1. Arrange the blocks as shown in the block layout and quilt plan. Join the blocks into rows; join the rows (page 15).
2. Fly-stitch (page 16) the seams if desired.
3. From the print scraps, cut seventy-six 2½" squares. Piece the squares to make 4 border strips: 2 strips of 18 squares each for the side borders and 2 strips of 20 squares each for the top and bottom borders.
4. Add the side borders; add the top and bottom borders (page 17).
5. Bind the edges using your favorite method or the appliquilt method (page 18).
6. Attach buttons as desired. Label your quilt.

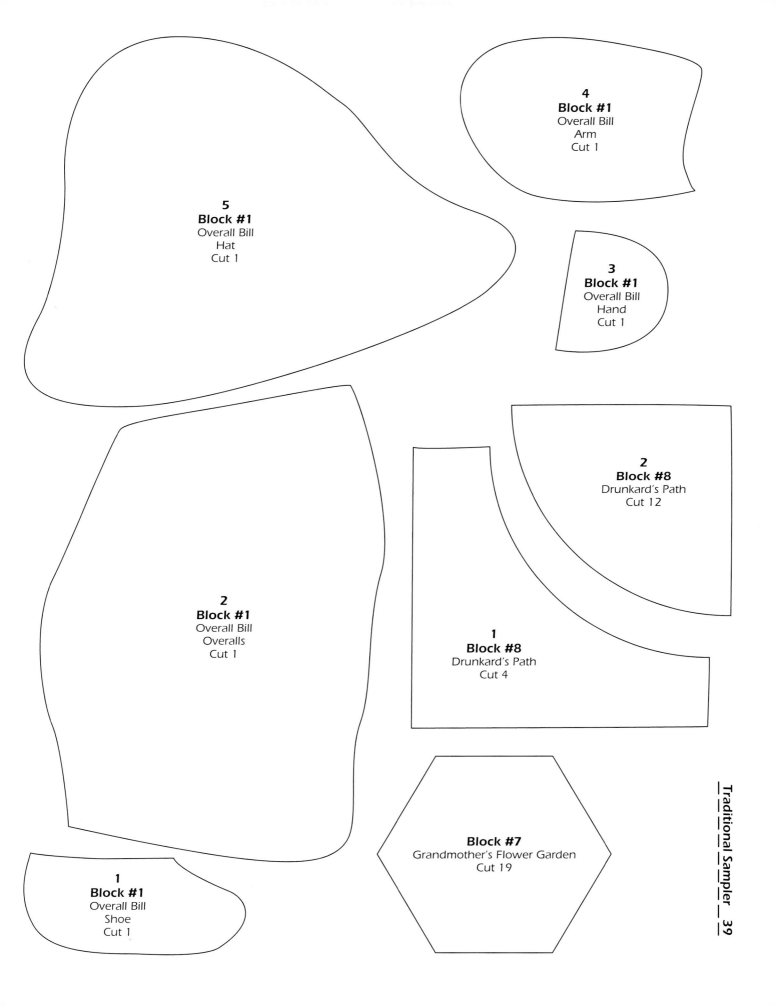

4
Block #1
Overall Bill
Arm
Cut 1

5
Block #1
Overall Bill
Hat
Cut 1

3
Block #1
Overall Bill
Hand
Cut 1

2
Block #8
Drunkard's Path
Cut 12

2
Block #1
Overall Bill
Overalls
Cut 1

1
Block #8
Drunkard's Path
Cut 4

Block #7
Grandmother's Flower Garden
Cut 19

1
Block #1
Overall Bill
Shoe
Cut 1

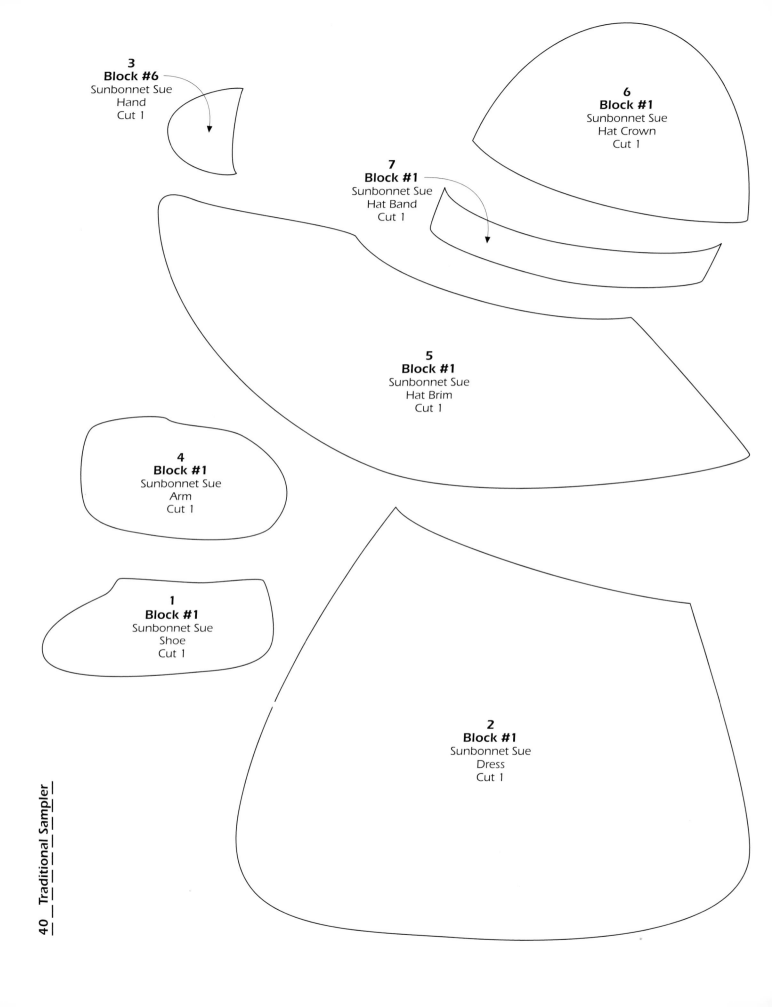

3
Block #6
Sunbonnet Sue
Hand
Cut 1

6
Block #1
Sunbonnet Sue
Hat Crown
Cut 1

7
Block #1
Sunbonnet Sue
Hat Band
Cut 1

5
Block #1
Sunbonnet Sue
Hat Brim
Cut 1

4
Block #1
Sunbonnet Sue
Arm
Cut 1

1
Block #1
Sunbonnet Sue
Shoe
Cut 1

2
Block #1
Sunbonnet Sue
Dress
Cut 1

Block #6
Fan
Cut 12

Block #4
Dutchman's Puzzle
Cut 8

1
Block #2
Basket Handle
Cut 4

2
Block #2
Basket
Cut 4

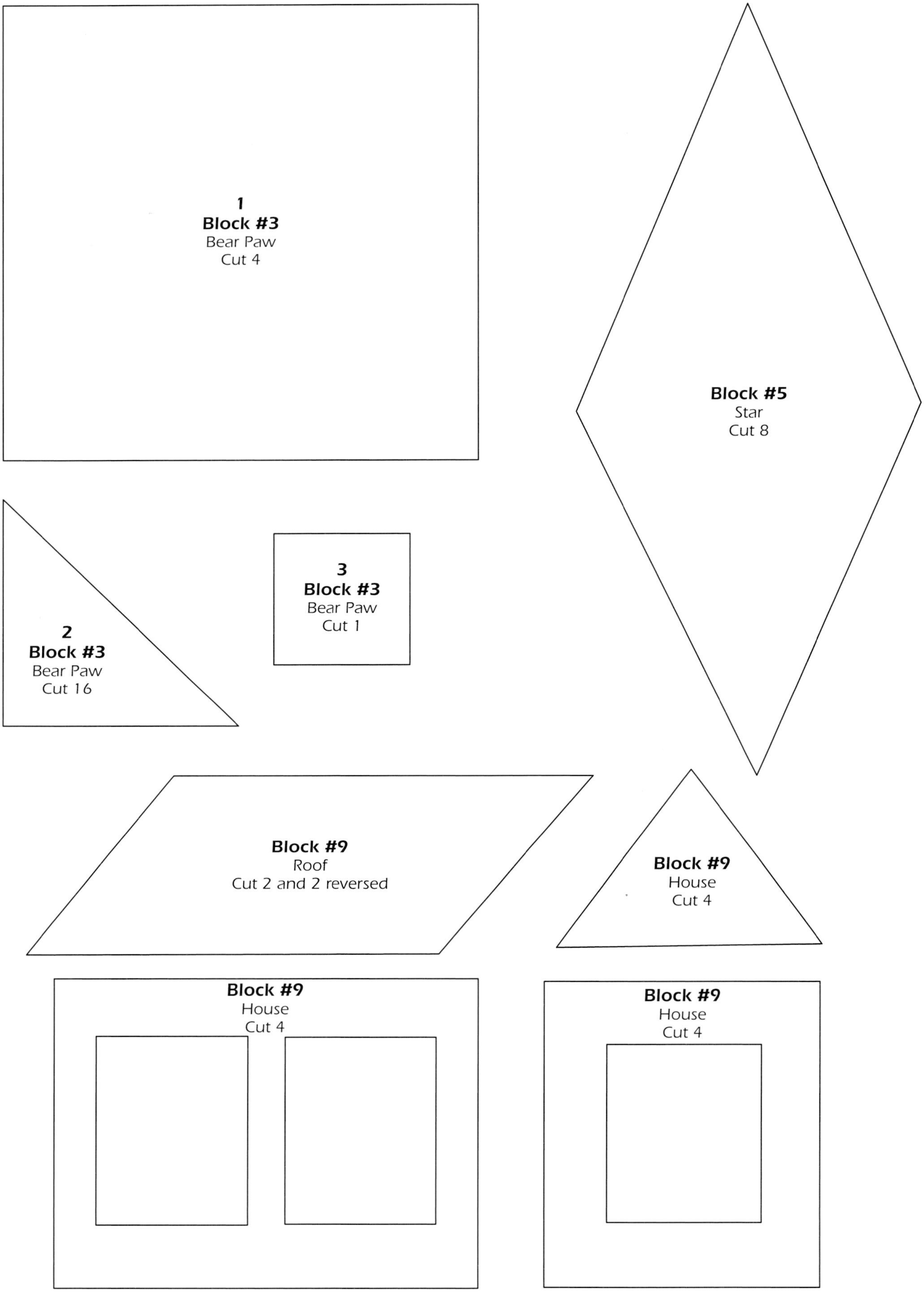

1
Block #3
Bear Paw
Cut 4

Block #5
Star
Cut 8

2
Block #3
Bear Paw
Cut 16

3
Block #3
Bear Paw
Cut 1

Block #9
Roof
Cut 2 and 2 reversed

Block #9
House
Cut 4

Block #9
House
Cut 4

Block #9
House
Cut 4

Apple Sampler

Traditional blocks and apple fixings combine for a cheery wall hanging.

Color photo: page 22
Size: 28" x 28"
Materials: 44"-wide fabric

⅝ yd. print #1 for center-block and corner-block backgrounds

⅜ yd. print #2 for middle-block background

¾ yd. Pellon fleece or other thin batting

1 yd. fabric for backing

⅜ yd. fabric for border

½ yd. total of assorted reds and greens for apples

Assorted scraps for pieced blocks and appliqué pieces

¼ yd. fabric for binding

Perle cotton in assorted colors

Green permanent marker

Buttons of your choice

Embellishments of your choice

Cutting

From print #1, cut:
    1 square, 9" x 9", for center block
    4 squares, each 8¾" x 8¾", for corner blocks

From print #2, cut:
    4 rectangles, each 8¾" x 9", for middle blocks

From the batting, cut:
    1 square, 8" x 8", for center block
    4 rectangles, each 8" x 10", for middle blocks
    4 squares, each 10" x 10", for corner blocks

From the backing fabric, cut:
    1 square, 9" x 9", for center block
    4 rectangles, each 9" x 10½", for middle blocks
    4 squares, each 10½" x 10½", for corner blocks

From the border fabric, cut:
    2 strips, each 2½" x 24½", for side borders
    2 strips, each 2½" x 28", for top and bottom borders

Making the Block Sandwiches

Refer to the instructions on pages 10–12 to layer and label the block sandwiches.

Appliquilting the Blocks

Use the templates on pages 45–47 and on the pullout pattern. Refer to the quilt plan for layout of the pieces. The numbers on the templates indicate the stitching order.

1. Make the templates and cut out the appliqué pieces, referring to the instructions on page 13.
2. Appliquilt the apples, quilt blocks, tree, jars, and pie, referring to the instructions on page 14. (Do not appliquilt the apple stems and leaves yet.) Special instructions for specific blocks follow.

Block #1	Block #2	Block #3
Block #4	Block #5	Block #6
Block #7	Block #8	Block #9

Block Layout Diagram

Block #1: Card Trick

Pink four 3" squares. Arrange the squares, overlapping the corners. Appliquilt in place.

Block #2: Tree

For the Nine Patch block behind the tree, cut five 2" squares from a red print and four 2" squares from a white print. Join the squares in 3 rows of 3 squares each, alternating the colors. Pink the edges. Appliquilt in an "X" pattern in the white squares.

Do not appliquilt the upper tree leaves until the blocks and border are joined.

Block #3: Jars

From muslin, cut 2 rectangles, one 1½" x 3" and the other 1⅛" x 2". Using a permanent marker, write "SAUCE" on the larger rectangle and "JAM" on the other. Appliquilt in place.

Block #4: Bow Tie

Pink two 2¼" light squares, two 2¼" dark squares, and one 1½" dark square. Arrange the 2¼" squares in a four-patch unit; appliquilt in place. To make a Bow Tie, place the 1½" square in the center, on point; appliquilt in place.

Block #6: Nine Patch

Cut 2½" squares and assemble as you did for Block #2. Pink the edges. Appliquilt in place.

Block #8: Log Cabin

Cut a 2" center square and 1¼"-wide strips. Assemble as shown; pink the edges. Appliquilt in place.

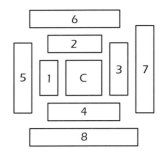

Assembling and Finishing the Quilt

1. Arrange the blocks as shown in the block layout and quilt plan. Join the blocks into rows; join the rows (page 15).
2. Fly-stitch (page 16) the seams if desired.
3. Add the side borders; add the top and bottom borders (page 17).
4. Appliquilt the apple stems and leaves and the upper tree leaves, overlapping the seams.
5. Bind the edges using your favorite method or the appliquilt method (page 18.)
6. Attach buttons as desired. Label your quilt.

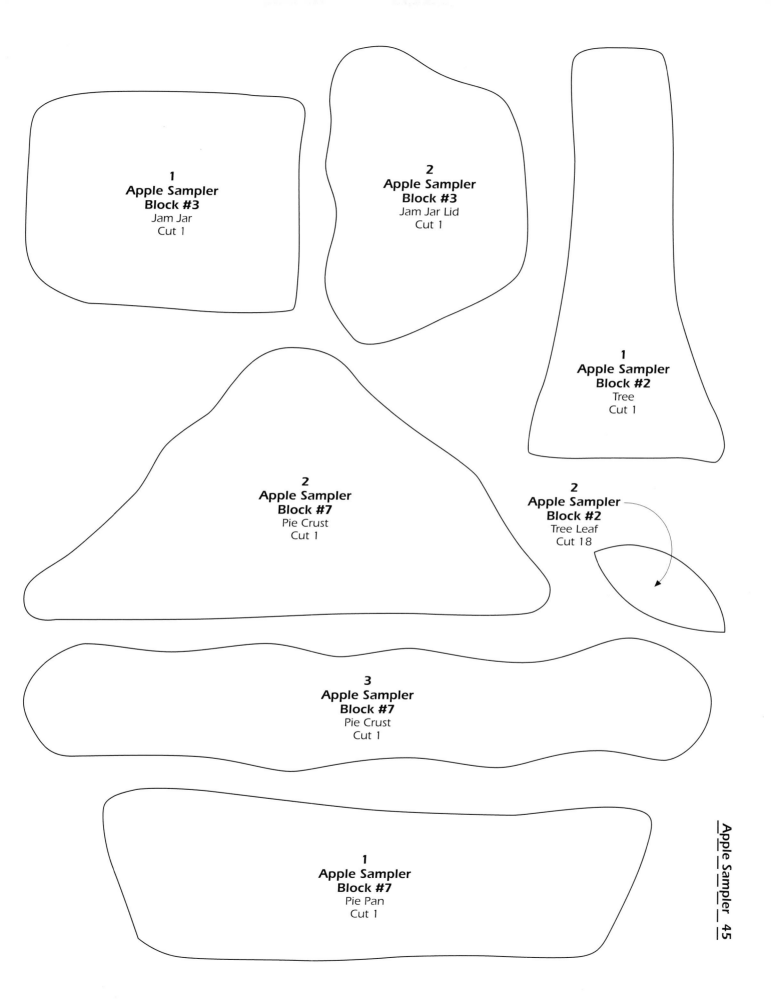

1
Apple Sampler
Block #3
Jam Jar
Cut 1

2
Apple Sampler
Block #3
Jam Jar Lid
Cut 1

1
Apple Sampler
Block #2
Tree
Cut 1

2
Apple Sampler
Block #7
Pie Crust
Cut 1

2
Apple Sampler
Block #2
Tree Leaf
Cut 18

3
Apple Sampler
Block #7
Pie Crust
Cut 1

1
Apple Sampler
Block #7
Pie Pan
Cut 1

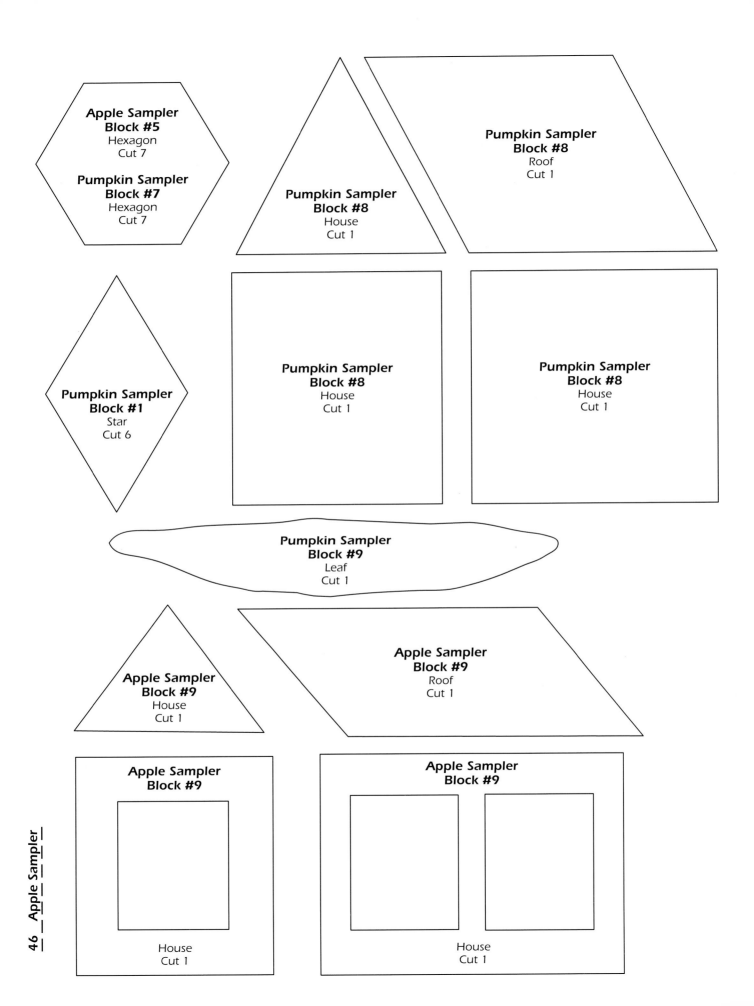

**Apple Sampler
Block #5**
Hexagon
Cut 7

**Pumpkin Sampler
Block #7**
Hexagon
Cut 7

**Pumpkin Sampler
Block #8**
House
Cut 1

**Pumpkin Sampler
Block #8**
Roof
Cut 1

**Pumpkin Sampler
Block #1**
Star
Cut 6

**Pumpkin Sampler
Block #8**
House
Cut 1

**Pumpkin Sampler
Block #8**
House
Cut 1

**Pumpkin Sampler
Block #9**
Leaf
Cut 1

**Apple Sampler
Block #9**
House
Cut 1

**Apple Sampler
Block #9**
Roof
Cut 1

**Apple Sampler
Block #9**

House
Cut 1

**Apple Sampler
Block #9**

House
Cut 1

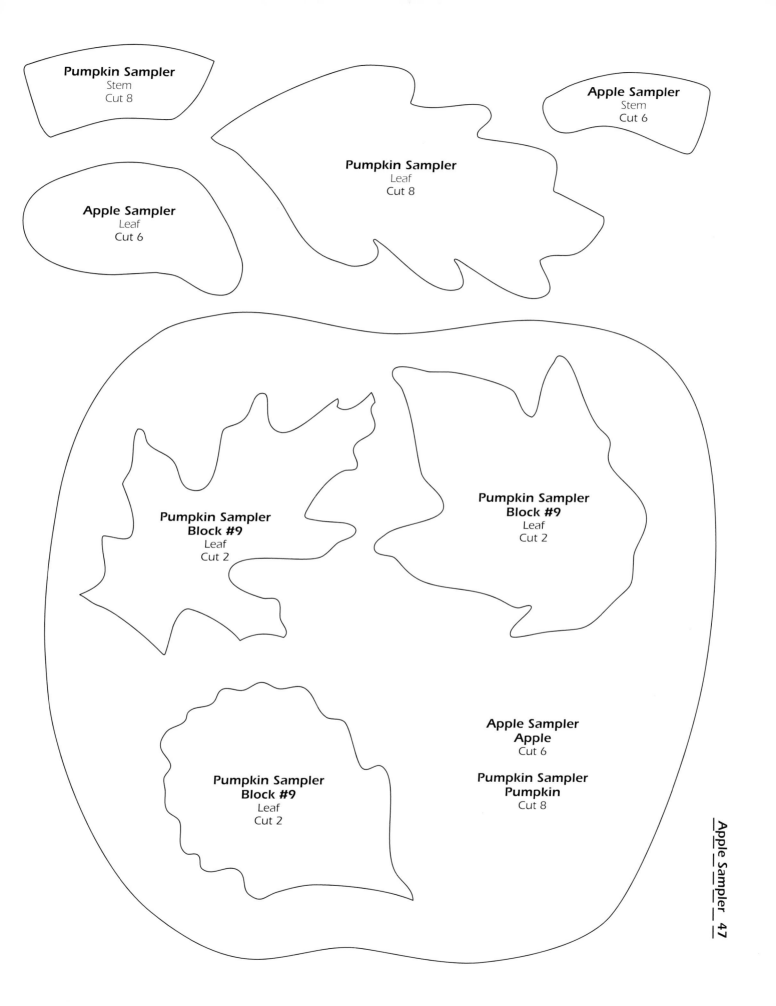

Pumpkin Sampler
Stem
Cut 8

Apple Sampler
Stem
Cut 6

Pumpkin Sampler
Leaf
Cut 8

Apple Sampler
Leaf
Cut 6

Pumpkin Sampler
Block #9
Leaf
Cut 2

Pumpkin Sampler
Block #9
Leaf
Cut 2

Pumpkin Sampler
Block #9
Leaf
Cut 2

Apple Sampler
Apple
Cut 6

Pumpkin Sampler
Pumpkin
Cut 8

Pumpkin Sampler

Autumn colors give this quilt a warm and cozy feeling. Stitch this quick and easy wall hanging to welcome fall.

Color photo: page 22
Size: 28" x 28"
Materials: 44"-wide fabric

⅝ yd. black solid for center-block and corner-block backgrounds

⅜ yd. stripe for middle-block background

¾ yd. Pellon fleece or other thin batting

1 yd. fabric for backing

⅜ yd. fabric for border

½ yd. total of assorted oranges for pumpkins

Assorted scraps for pieced blocks and appliqué pieces

¼ yd. fabric for binding

Perle cotton in assorted colors

Buttons of your choice

Cutting

From the black solid, cut:
  1 square, 9" x 9", for center block
  4 squares, each 8¾" x 8¾", for corner blocks

From the stripe, cut:
  4 rectangles, each 8¾" x 9", for middle blocks

From the batting, cut:
  1 square, 8" x 8", for center block
  4 rectangles, each 8" x 10", for middle blocks
  4 squares, each 10" x 10", for corner blocks

From the backing fabric, cut:
  1 square, 9" x 9", for center block
  4 rectangles, each 9" x 10½", for middle blocks
  4 squares, each 10½" x 10½", for corner blocks

From the border fabric, cut:
  2 strips, each 2½" x 24½", for side borders
  2 strips, each 2½" x 28", for top and bottom borders

Making the Block Sandwiches

Refer to the instructions on pages 10–12 to layer and label the block sandwiches.

Appliquilting the Blocks

Use the templates on pages 46–47. Refer to the quilt plan for layout of the pieces. The numbers on the templates indicate the stitching order.

1. Make the templates and cut out the appliqué pieces, referring to the instructions on page 13.
2. Appliquilt the pumpkins and quilt blocks, referring to the instructions on page 14. (Do not appliquilt the pumpkin stems and leaves yet.) Special instructions for specific blocks follow.

Block #1	Block #2	Block #3
Block #4	Block #5	Block #6
Block #7	Block #8	Block #9

Block Layout Diagram

Block #1: Star

Appliquilt 6 diamonds, alternating light and dark pieces. Overlap the pieces to prevent the background from showing.

Block #2: Sixteen Patch

Cut four 1¼" squares from each of four different colors. Sew the squares together in four rows of four squares each, arranging the colors as shown in the photo. Pink the edges. Appliquilt in place.

Block #3: Nine Patch

Cut five 2" squares from a medium print and four 2" squares from a light print. Sew the squares together in 3 rows of 3 blocks each, alternating the colors. Pink the edges. Appliquilt in a large "X" pattern.

Block #4: Square-in-a-Square

Pink a 3" square. Pink a 3½" square twice diagonally to make 4 triangles. Appliquilt in place.

3½"

Block #5: Log Cabin

See Block #8, "Apple Sampler" (page 44).

Block #6: Bow Tie

See Block #4, "Apple Sampler" (page 44).

Block #9: Leaves

Arrange the leaves on the background. Appliquilt in place.

Assembling and Finishing the Quilt

1. Arrange the blocks as shown in the block layout and quilt plan. Join the blocks into rows; join the rows (page 15).
2. Fly-stitch (page 16) the seams if desired.
3. Add the side borders; add the top and bottom borders (page 17).
4. Appliquilt the pumpkin stems and leaves, overlapping the seams.
5. Bind the edges using your favorite method or the appliquilt method (page 18).
6. Attach buttons as desired. Label your quilt.

Easter Sampler

Bunnies, chicks, and Easter eggs come together in this bright celebration of spring.

Color photo: page 25
Size: 40" x 40"
Materials: 44"-wide fabric

⅞ yd. solid fabric for center-block and corner-block background

⅞ yd. stripe fabric for middle-block background

⅓ yd. green plaid for house background

1⅓ yds. Pellon fleece or other thin batting

1¾ yds. fabric for backing

½ yd. fabric for border and binding

⅓ yd. brown print for basket

Assorted scraps for remaining appliqué pieces

Perle cotton in assorted colors

⅞"-wide gathered eyelet for girl bunny

Narrow ribbon for girl bunny

4 large and 4 extra-large yellow pom-pons for chicks

4 mini pink pom-pons and 4 small white pom-pons for bunnies

Tiny plastic eyes for chicks

Orange felt scrap and orange thread for chick beaks

Fusible web

Embroidery floss

Linen thread

Buttons of your choice

Embellishments of your choice, such as miniature vegetables, basket, and rabbit pin

Cutting

From the solid background fabric, cut:
  1 rectangle, 5¼" x 13", for center block
  4 squares, each 12¾" x 12¾", for corner blocks

From the stripe, cut:
  4 rectangles, each 12¾" x 13", for middle blocks

From the green plaid, cut:
  1 rectangle, 8¼" x 13", for center block. Using a ¼"-wide seam allowance, stitch the solid and green plaid background rectangles together to make a 13" square for the center-block background.

From the batting, cut:
  1 square, 12" x 12", for center block
  4 rectangles, each 12" x 14", for middle blocks
  4 squares, each 14" x 14", for corner blocks

From the backing fabric, cut:
  1 square, 13" x 13", for center block
  4 rectangles, each 13" x 14½", for middle blocks
  4 squares, each 14½" x 14½", for corner blocks

From the border fabric, cut:
  2 strips, each 2½" x 36½", for side borders
  2 strips, each 2½" x 40", for top and bottom borders

Making the Block Sandwiches

Refer to the instructions on pages 10–12 to layer and label the block sandwiches.

Appliquilting the Blocks

Use the templates on pages 52–54 and the pull-out pattern. Refer to the quilt plan for layout of the pieces. The numbers on the templates indicate the stitching order.
  1. Make the templates and cut out the appliqué pieces, referring to the instructions on page 13.
  2. Appliquilt the pieces, referring to the instructions on page 14. Special instructions for specific blocks follow.

Block #1	Block #2	Block #3
Block #4	Block #5	Block #6
Block #7	Block #8	Block #9

Block Layout Diagram

Block #1: Carrots

For the large carrot tops, pink twelve ¼" x 14" strips of green fabric. Place 3 strips under the wide end of each large carrot. Appliquilt the carrots, catching the ends of the strips in the stitching. Tack the strips to the block with square knots.

Place a small carrot top under the wide end of each small carrot. Appliquilt in place.

Block #2: Basket

1. Following the instructions on page 20 for three-dimensional shapes, make the basket and 5 eggs.
2. Cut a strip of fabric 2¼" wide and the width of the fabric. Tie the strip into a bow.
3. Arrange the pieces on the block sandwich, eggs first, then the napkin and the basket. Tack each egg in place with a square knot. The knot will be hidden by the napkin.
4. Appliquilt the basket on the outer and inner edges as indicated on the template. Tack the basket to the block with a square knot at the point marked "X" on the template.
5. Attach the bow to the handle and tack the ends with square knots.

Block #4: Girl Bunny

1. Arrange the girl bunny pieces, placing the eyelet under the sleeves and the dress hem. Appliquilt in place.
2. Make the three-dimensional ears (page 20). Cut 2 pieces of ribbon and tie into bows. Tack the bows and the ears to the head with square knots.
3. Cut four 3" strands of linen thread and stitch them under the nose. Using a backstitch (page 20) and 3 strands of embroidery floss, stitch the mouth. Attach small buttons for the eyes.

Block #5: Peter's Home

1. Appliquilt the pieces in place, except for the tree top. Appliquilt the tree top in place after the blocks are joined.
2. Using a permanent marker, write "PETER" on the house sign.
3. "Plant" the garden patch using 3 strands of green embroidery floss and straight stitches. (See Resources on page 9 for the jelly bean buttons.)

Block #6: Boy Bunny

1. Arrange the boy bunny pieces, except for the ears and hat. Appliquilt in place.
2. Make the three-dimensional ears (page 20). Tack the ears in place; appliquilt the hat over the ears.
3. Stitch the face as you did on the Girl Bunny block.

Block #7: Chicks

1. Make 4 three-dimensional cracked eggs (page 20). Appliquilt, leaving the top edge of the eggs unstitched.
2. To make each chick, sew 1 large and 1 extra-large pom-pon together using a long darning needle. Glue 2 eyes to each large pom-pon. Make a total of 4 chicks.

3. Cut out 4 beaks from orange felt. Place each beak below the eyes and, using a darning needle and orange thread, stitch the beak with 2 stitches that run through the pom-pon.

Stitches

4. Pull the thread tight to make the felt fold in the middle. Place the chicks in the eggs and tack to the block.

Block #8: Carrot Stew

Using fusible web and following the manufacturer's directions, fuse the letters to the stew pot. Attach the miniature vegetables.

Block #9: Bunny Circle

Attach mini pink pom-pons for the noses and small white pom-pons for the tails. For the eyes, make French knots (page 20) using 3 strands of embroidery floss wrapped once around the needle.

Assembling and Finishing the Quilt

1. Arrange the blocks as shown in the block layout and quilt plan. Join the blocks into rows; join the rows (page 15).
2. Fly-stitch (page 16) the seams if desired.
3. Appliquilt the tree top to the house block, overlapping the seam. Tack the remaining carrot tops, overlapping the seams.
4. Add the side borders; add the top and bottom borders (page 17).
5. Bind the edges using your favorite method or the appliquilt method (page 18).
6. Attach buttons as desired. Label your quilt.

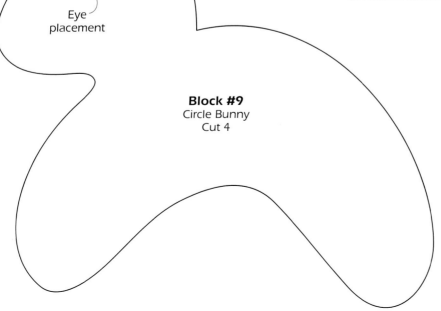

Eye placement

Block #9
Circle Bunny
Cut 4

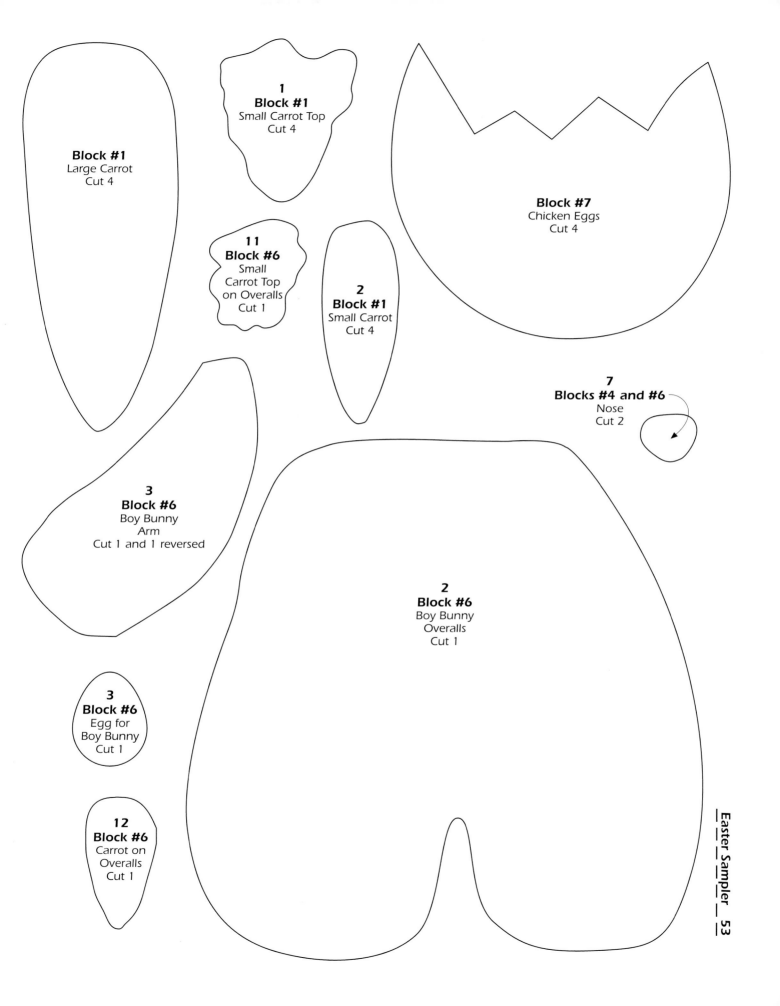

Block #1
Large Carrot
Cut 4

1
Block #1
Small Carrot Top
Cut 4

11
Block #6
Small
Carrot Top
on Overalls
Cut 1

2
Block #1
Small Carrot
Cut 4

Block #7
Chicken Eggs
Cut 4

7
Blocks #4 and #6
Nose
Cut 2

3
Block #6
Boy Bunny
Arm
Cut 1 and 1 reversed

2
Block #6
Boy Bunny
Overalls
Cut 1

3
Block #6
Egg for
Boy Bunny
Cut 1

12
Block #6
Carrot on
Overalls
Cut 1

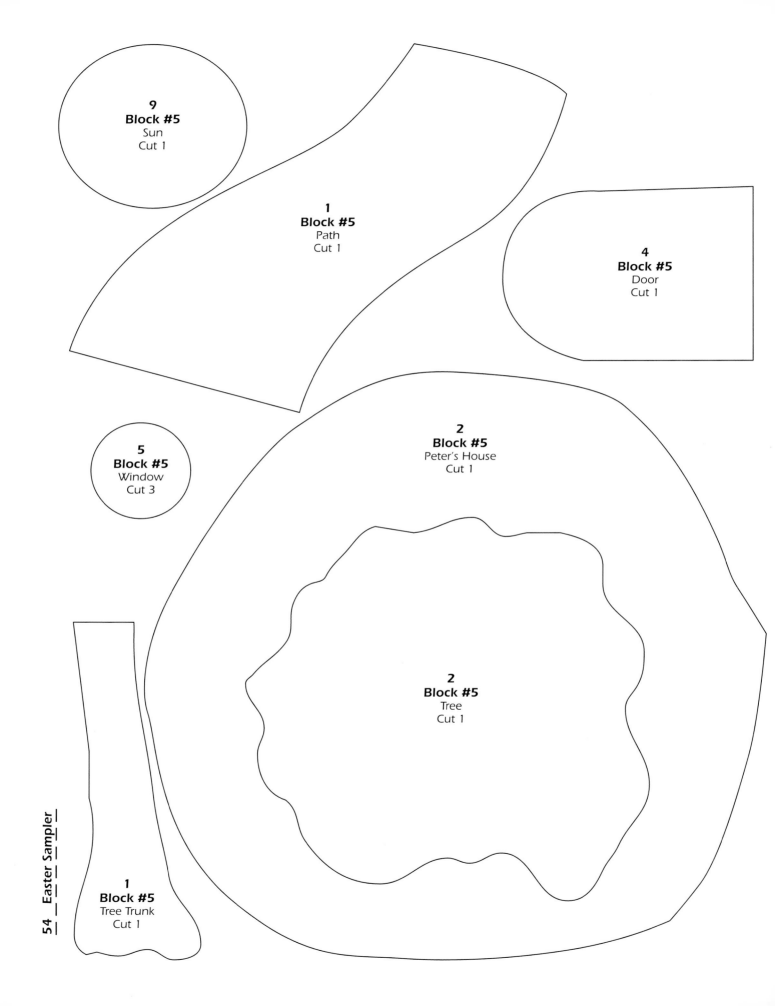

9
Block #5
Sun
Cut 1

1
Block #5
Path
Cut 1

4
Block #5
Door
Cut 1

5
Block #5
Window
Cut 3

2
Block #5
Peter's House
Cut 1

2
Block #5
Tree
Cut 1

1
Block #5
Tree Trunk
Cut 1

A Country Sampling

A collection of Country motifs come together in this generous twelve-block wall hanging. Make it the focal point of your favorite room.

Color photo: page 27
Size: 40" x 52"
Materials: 44"-wide fabric

½ yd. total of 3 dark fabrics for background

1¼ yds. total of 9 light fabrics for background

1½ yds. Pellon fleece or other thin batting

1¾ yds. fabric for backing

7" square of bandanna fabric for bear

⅓ yd. gold solid for sunflower

¼ yd. black check for sunflower center

¼ yd. check for pig

Assorted scraps for remaining appliqué pieces and borders

10" square of Osnaberg or tea-dyed muslin for ABCs

¼ yd. fabric for binding

Perle cotton in assorted colors

Embroidery floss in assorted colors

Jute for hearts and pig

Cotton doll hair for angel

Buttons of your choice

Embellishments of your choice, such as ribbons, beads, spools, charms, and lace

Cutting

From the background fabrics, cut:

> 2 squares, each 13" x 13", for center blocks
> 6 rectangles, each 12¾" x 13", for middle blocks
> 4 squares, each 12¾" x 12¾", for corner blocks

From the batting, cut:

> 2 squares, each 12" x 12", for center blocks
> 6 rectangles, each 12" x 14", for middle blocks
> 4 squares, each 14" x 14", for corner blocks

From the backing fabric, cut:

> 2 squares, each 13" x 13", for center blocks
> 6 rectangles, each 13" x 14½", for middle blocks
> 4 squares, each 14½" x 14½", for corner blocks

From the scraps, cut:

> Enough 2½"-wide strips to make two 48½"-long strips, for side borders
> Enough 2½"-wide strips to make two 40"-long strips, for top and bottom borders

Making the Block Sandwiches

Refer to the instructions on pages 10–12 to layer and label the block sandwiches.

Appliquilting the Blocks

Use the templates on pages 58–61 and the pull-out pattern. Refer to the quilt plan for layout of the pieces. The numbers on the templates indicate the stitching order.

1. Make the templates and cut out the appliqué pieces, referring to the instructions on page 13.
2. Appliquilt the pieces, referring to the instructions on page 14. Special instructions for specific blocks follow.

Block #1	Block #2	Block #3
Block #4	Block #5	Block #6
Block #7	Block #8	Block #9
Block #10	Block #11	Block #12

Block Layout Diagram

Block #1: Bear

1. Pink a 6½" square for the bear's bandanna. Fold the square diagonally and, using perle cotton, stitch the raw edges together.
2. With the folded edge of the bandanna at the bear's neck, draw up the corners and tack in place as shown. Sew a button to the lower corner of the bandanna.

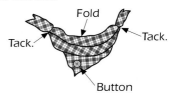

Block #2: Angel

Pink a 4" x 6" piece of striped fabric and a 2" x 3½" piece of star fabric for the angel's flag. Appliquilt in place. Arrange the doll hair; tack.

Block #6: Pig

1. Pink a ½ x 8" strip of fabric for the pig's pull toy. Appliquilt in place.
2. Make 2 yo-yos (page 19) for the wheels. Stitch the yo-yos to the block with buttons.
3. Cut an 11" length of jute. Attach it to the front of the pull toy with a button. Thread a wooden bead on the other end and tack it to the block.
4. Pink a ½" x 3" piece of pig fabric. Attach one end to the pig with a square knot. Twist the strip twice and tack it to the block.

Block #7: Numbers

Draw a nine-square grid on the block sandwich. Appliquilt on the lines before appliquilting the pieces.

Block #8: Apples

Draw a four-square grid on the block sandwich. Appliquilt on the lines before appliquilting the pieces.

Block #9: House

Using 3 strands of embroidery floss and a running stitch, outline smoke rising from the chimney.

Block #10: Quilts

Make mini quilts using fabric printed in patchwork patterns. Paper foundation piecing is another option. The mini quilts in the photo measure 4½" x 4½", 5" x 6½", and 4" x 4". Layer each mini quilt top with backing fabric (without batting) and bind the edges. Tack the mini quilts to the block from the back, being careful not to catch the front.

Block #11: Pitcher

1. For the picture frame, pink a 4" square of fabric. Using a rubber stamp, a small piece of cross-stitch, or a motif cut from printed fabric, create a 3" picture square. Appliquilt the picture and frame.
2. Cut two 8" lengths of narrow ribbon. Tack the ends to the upper corners of the frame. Tie the free ends in a bow and tack the bow to the block.

Block #12: Sampler

1. Fray the edges of the 10" square of Osnaberg or tea-dyed muslin. Use a transfer pen and follow the manufacturer's instructions, or trace the alphabet onto the square.
2. Using 3 strands of embroidery floss, backstitch (page 20) the letters, flowers, and numbers. Appliquilt the square.

Assembling and Finishing the Quilt

1. Arrange the blocks as shown in the block layout and quilt plan. Join the blocks into rows; join the rows (page 15).
2. Fly-stitch (page 16) the seams if desired.
3. To make the scrap borders, piece varying lengths of 2½"-wide strips to make 2 strips, each 48½" long, for the sides, and 2 strips, each 40½" long, for the top and bottom. Add the side borders; then add the top and bottom borders (page 17).
4. Bind the edges using your favorite method or the appliquilt method (page 18).
5. Attach buttons as desired. Label your quilt.

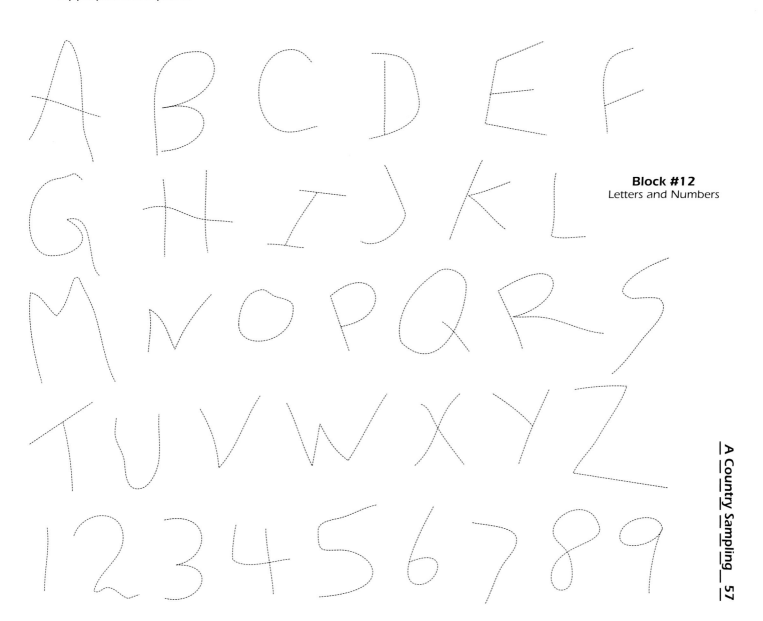

Block #12
Letters and Numbers

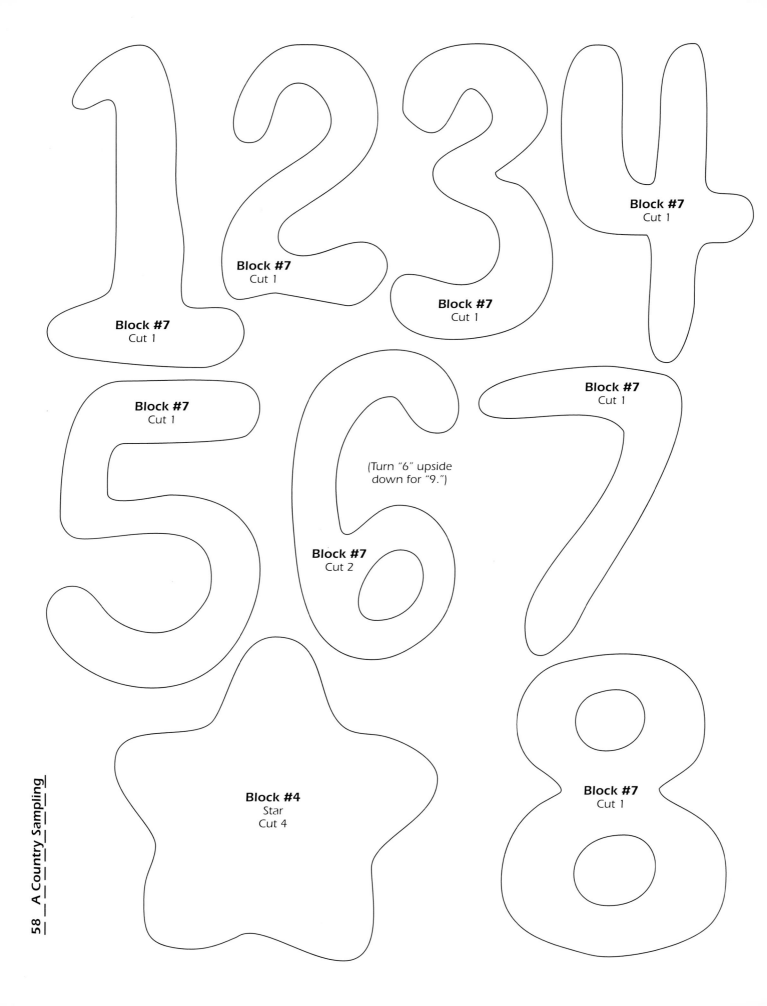

Block #7
Cut 1

Block #7
Cut 1

Block #7
Cut 1

Block #7
Cut 1

Block #7
Cut 1

Block #7
Cut 1

(Turn "6" upside down for "9.")

Block #7
Cut 2

Block #4
Star
Cut 4

Block #7
Cut 1

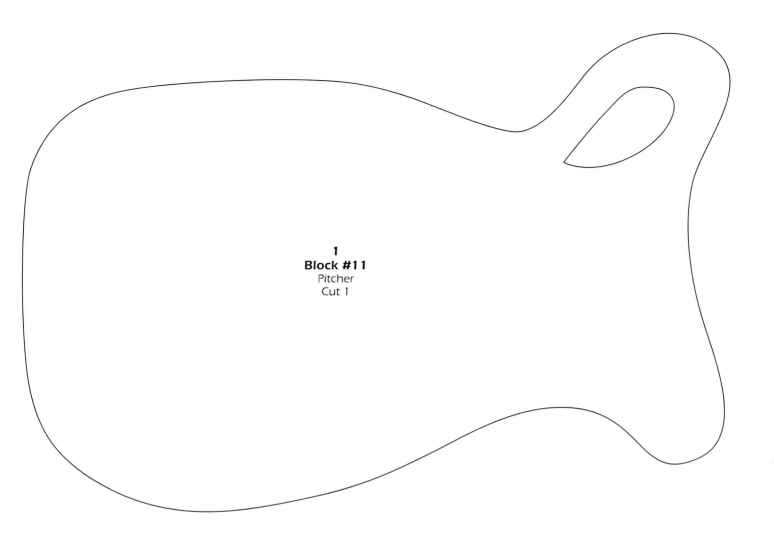

1
Block #11
Pitcher
Cut 1

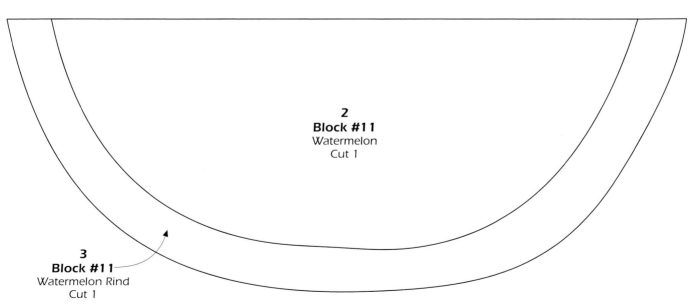

2
Block #11
Watermelon
Cut 1

3
Block #11
Watermelon Rind
Cut 1

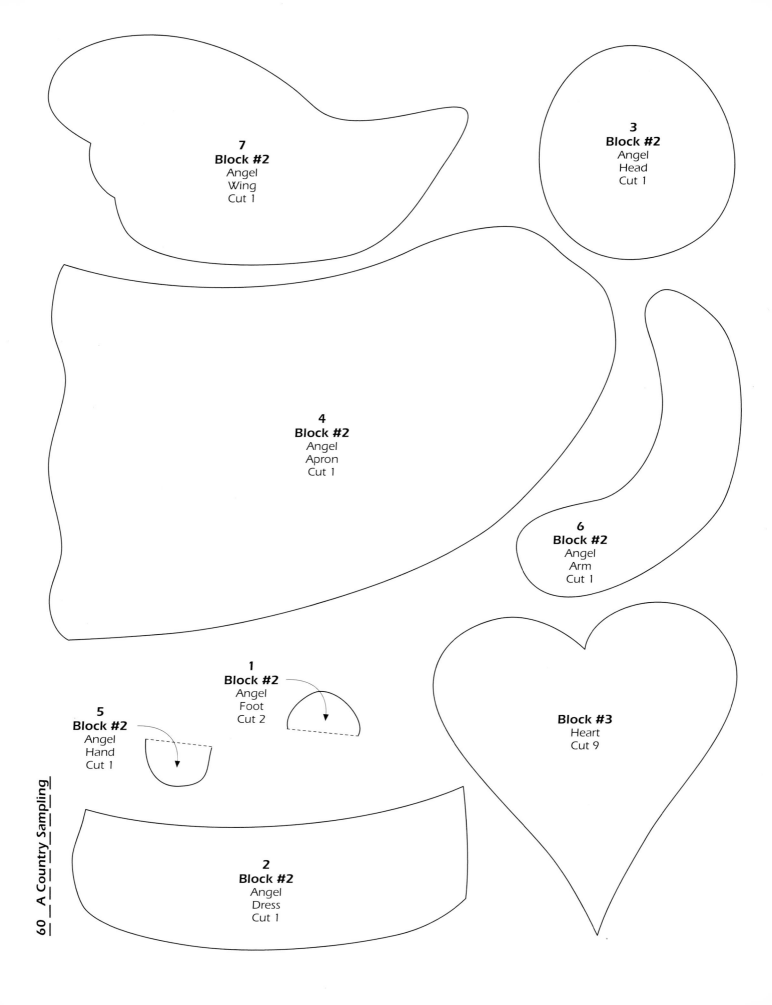

7
Block #2
Angel
Wing
Cut 1

3
Block #2
Angel
Head
Cut 1

4
Block #2
Angel
Apron
Cut 1

6
Block #2
Angel
Arm
Cut 1

1
Block #2
Angel
Foot
Cut 2

5
Block #2
Angel
Hand
Cut 1

Block #3
Heart
Cut 9

2
Block #2
Angel
Dress
Cut 1

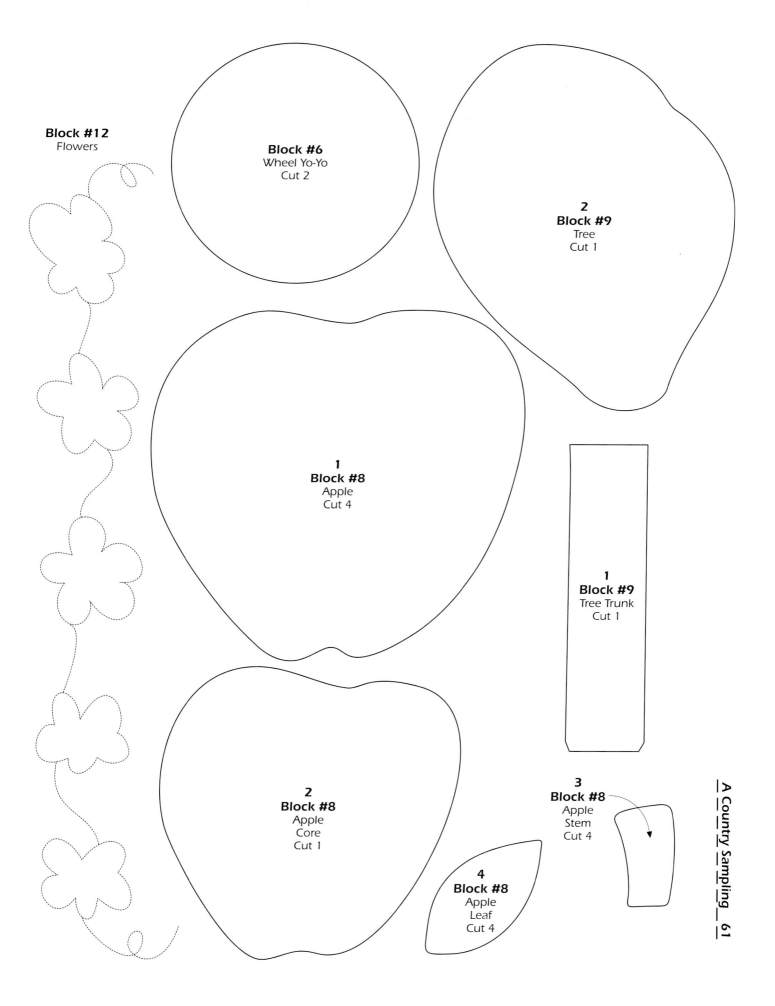

Block #12
Flowers

Block #6
Wheel Yo-Yo
Cut 2

2
Block #9
Tree
Cut 1

1
Block #8
Apple
Cut 4

1
Block #9
Tree Trunk
Cut 1

2
Block #8
Apple
Core
Cut 1

3
Block #8
Apple
Stem
Cut 4

4
Block #8
Apple
Leaf
Cut 4

Baltimore Album

The traditional Baltimore Album quilt is easy to make the appliquilt way.

Color photo: page 24
Size: 34" x 34"
Materials: 44"-wide fabric

1⅛ yds. off-white solid for background and binding

1⅛ yds. fabric for backing

1 yd. Pellon fleece or other thin batting

½ yd. blue solid for appliqué pieces

Scraps: ⅛ yd. each of cream, beige, brown, yellow, red, and green solids for appliqué pieces

Perle cotton in off-white and colors to match fabrics

Jute for anchor

Buttons and embellishments of your choice, such as black bird for Tree block

Cutting

From the off-white solid and backing fabric each, cut:
> 1 square, 10" x 10", for center block
> 4 rectangles, each 10" x 13", for middle blocks
> 4 squares, each 13" x 13", for corner blocks

From the batting, cut:
> 1 square, 9" x 9", for center block
> 4 rectangles, each 9" x 12½", for middle blocks
> 4 squares, each 12½" x 12½", for corner blocks

Making the Block Sandwiches

Refer to the instructions on pages 10–12 to layer and label the block sandwiches. **Note that this quilt has no borders.** When assembling the quilt, you won't see exposed batting on the perimeter of the corner and middle blocks.

Appliquilting the Blocks

Use the templates on pages 64–67 and the pull-out pattern. Refer to the quilt plan for layout of the pieces. The numbers on the templates indicate the stitching order.

1. Make the templates and cut out the appliqué pieces, referring to the instructions on page 13.
2. Appliquilt the pieces, referring to the instructions on page 14. Special instructions for specific blocks follow.

Block #1	Block #2	Block #3
Block #4	Block #5	Block #6
Block #7	Block #8	Block #9

Block Layout Diagram

Block #1: Tree

For the tree top, pink eight ¼"-wide strips of green fabric on the bias, making the strips 4½" to 6" long. Arrange the strips on top of the tree trunk, overlapping the ends. Appliquilt in place.

Block #2: Lute

Using 3 strands of embroidery floss, backstitch (page 20) the lute strings.

Block #3: Anchor

For the anchor, cut a 25" length of jute and arrange it so that one section lies under the anchor and one end runs through the anchor eye. Appliquilt the anchor.

Block #9: Basket

Make 3 yo-yos (page 19) and attach them to the block with buttons.

Assembling and Finishing the Quilt

1. Arrange the blocks as shown in the block layout and quilt plan. Join the blocks into rows; join the rows (page 15).
2. Cross-stitch (page 16) the seams if desired.
3. Arrange the swags and bows near the edges; appliquilt in place.
4. Bind the edges using your favorite method or the appliquilt method (page 18).
5. Attach buttons as desired. Label your quilt.

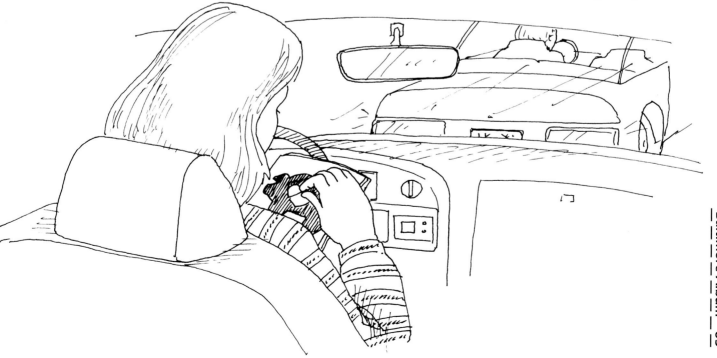

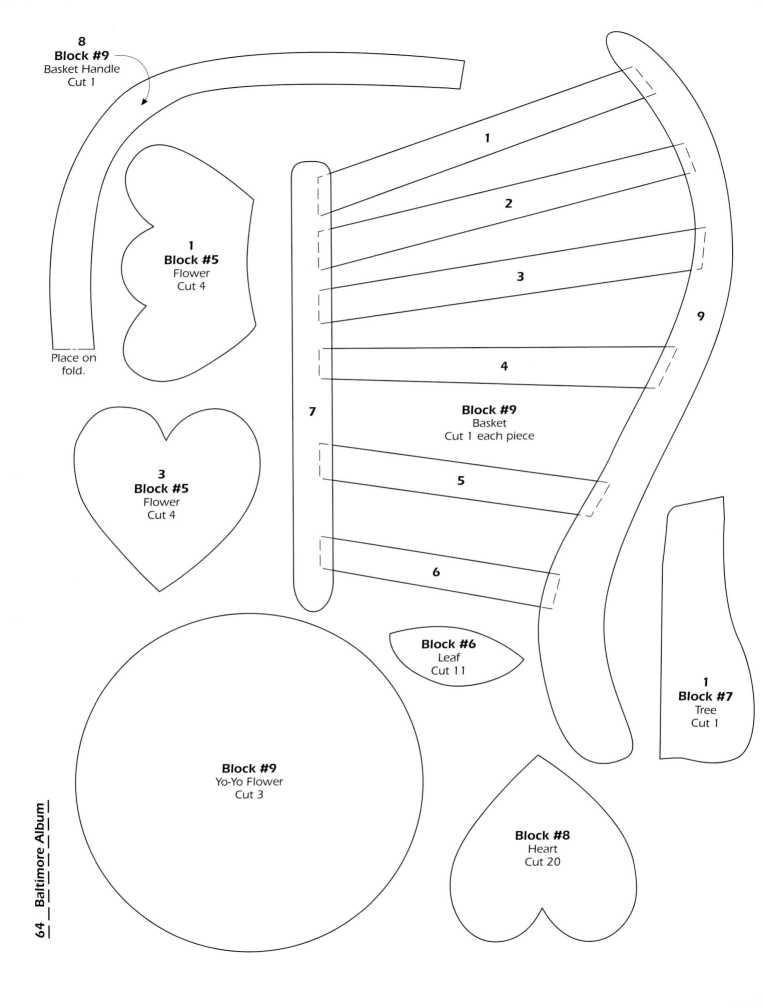

8
Block #9
Basket Handle
Cut 1

1
Block #5
Flower
Cut 4

Place on fold.

3
Block #5
Flower
Cut 4

1

2

3

9

4

7

Block #9
Basket
Cut 1 each piece

5

6

Block #6
Leaf
Cut 11

1
Block #7
Tree
Cut 1

Block #9
Yo-Yo Flower
Cut 3

Block #8
Heart
Cut 20

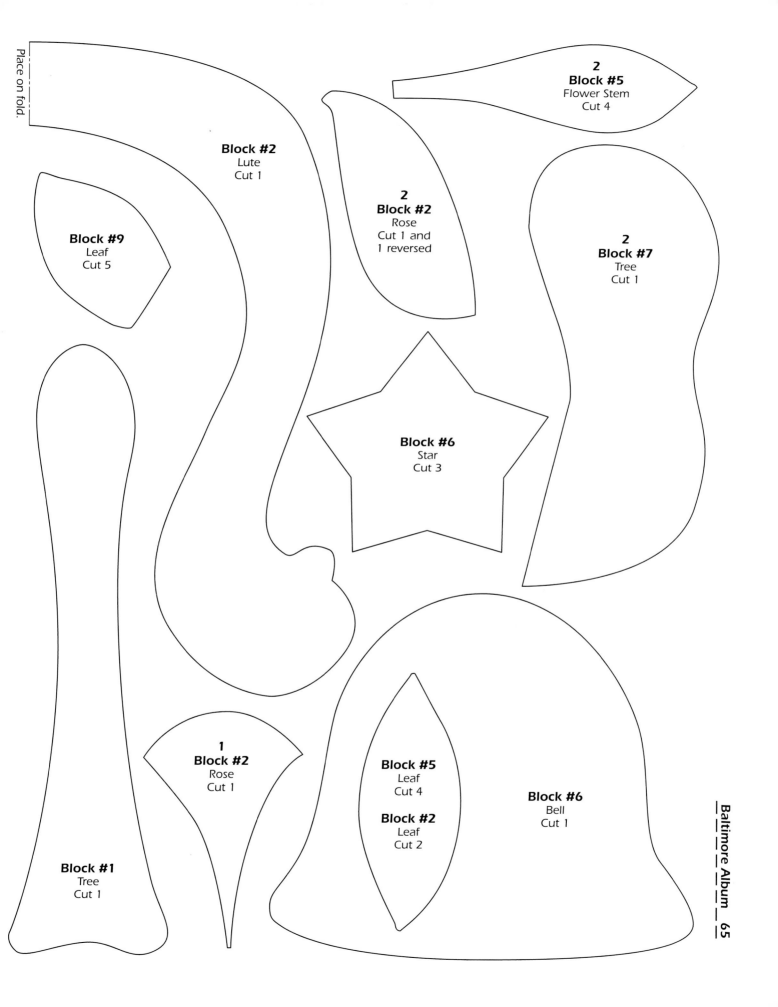

Place on fold.

Block #2
Lute
Cut 1

2
Block #5
Flower Stem
Cut 4

Block #9
Leaf
Cut 5

2
Block #2
Rose
Cut 1 and
1 reversed

2
Block #7
Tree
Cut 1

Block #6
Star
Cut 3

1
Block #2
Rose
Cut 1

Block #5
Leaf
Cut 4

Block #2
Leaf
Cut 2

Block #6
Bell
Cut 1

Block #1
Tree
Cut 1

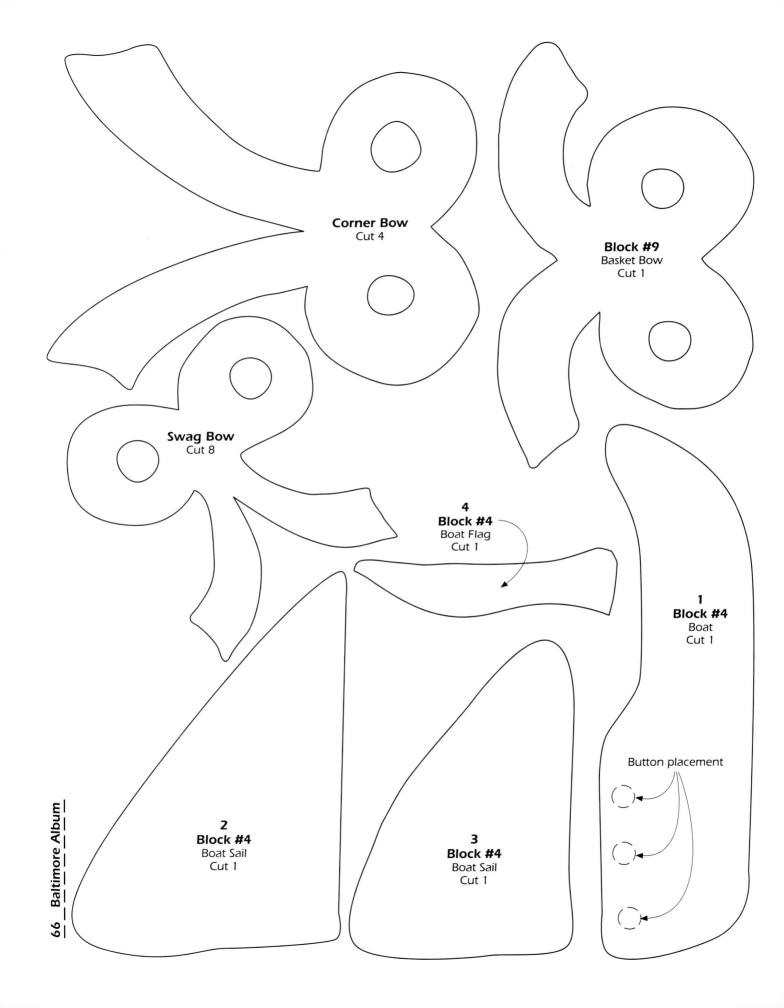

Corner Bow
Cut 4

Block #9
Basket Bow
Cut 1

Swag Bow
Cut 8

4
Block #4
Boat Flag
Cut 1

1
Block #4
Boat
Cut 1

Button placement

2
Block #4
Boat Sail
Cut 1

3
Block #4
Boat Sail
Cut 1

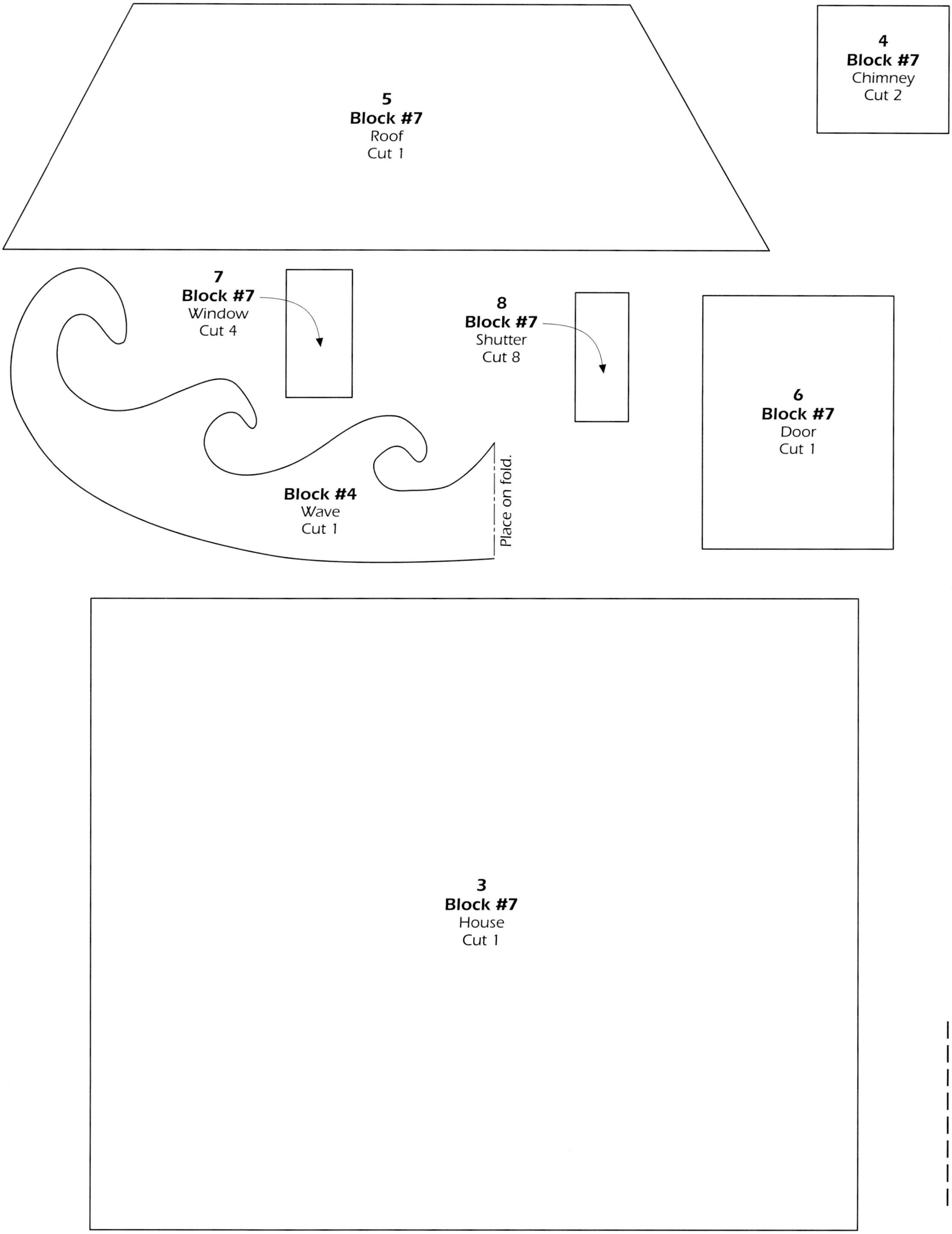

4
Block #7
Chimney
Cut 2

5
Block #7
Roof
Cut 1

7
Block #7
Window
Cut 4

8
Block #7
Shutter
Cut 8

Block #4
Wave
Cut 1

Place on fold.

6
Block #7
Door
Cut 1

3
Block #7
House
Cut 1

Baskets, Etc.

Stitch this fine collection of flower-filled baskets plus a basket of apples thrown in for interest. The crooked fence, complete with a small hanging basket, makes a great garden backdrop.

Color photo: page 26
Size: 44" x 44"
Materials: 44"-wide fabric

3/8 yd. yellow print for center-block background

7/8 yd. off-white solid for middle-block background

7/8 yd. yellow solid for corner-block background

1 1/3 yds. Pellon fleece or other thin batting

1 7/8 yds. fabric for backing

1/8 yd. fabric for inner border

2/3 yd. fabric for outer border

1/4 yd. each of 6 different prints for baskets

1/4 yd. wood-grain print for fence

Assorted scraps for remaining appliqué pieces

1/4 yd. fabric for binding

Perle cotton in assorted colors

Jute for basket handle

Buttons of your choice

Embellishments of your choice, such as lace doilies, ribbon roses, and costume jewelry

Cutting

From the yellow print, cut:
    1 square, 13" x 13", for center block

From the off-white solid, cut
    4 rectangles, each 13" x 12¾", for middle blocks

From the yellow solid, cut:
    4 squares, each 12 ¾" x 12¾", for corner blocks

From the batting, cut:
    1 square, 12" x 12", for center block
    4 rectangles, each 12" x 16", for middle blocks
    4 squares, each 16" x 16", for corner blocks

From the backing fabric, cut:
    1 square, 13" x 13", for center block
    4 rectangles, each 13" x 16½", for middle blocks
    4 squares, each 16½" x 16½" for corner blocks

From the inner border fabric, cut:
    4 strips, each 1" x 42"

From the outer border fabric, cut:
    2 strips, each 4½" x 36½", for side borders
    2 strips, each 4½" x 44", for top and bottom borders*

Piece strips for the necessary length.

Making the Block Sandwiches

Refer to the instructions on pages 10–12 to layer and label the block sandwiches.

Appliquilting the Blocks

Use the templates on pages 71–83 and the pull-out pattern. Refer to the quilt plan for layout of the pieces. The numbers on the templates indicate the stitching order.

1. Make the templates and cut out the appliqué pieces, referring to the instructions on page 13.
2. Appliquilt the pieces, referring to the instructions on page 14. Special instructions for specific blocks follow.

Block #1	Block #2	Block #3
Block #4	Block #5	Block #6
Block #7	Block #8	Block #9

Block Layout Diagram

Block #1

1. Pink ¼" x 30" strips of green fabric for the stems. Appliquilt down the middle of each stem, cutting the stems to the desired lengths as you stitch.
2. For the double yo-yo flowers, make large (outer) and medium (inner) yo-yos, using the templates on pages 73 and 77. Attach the large yo-yos, gathered side up, to the block (page 20); attach the medium yo-yos, gathered side down, on top of the large yo-yos.

   For the flower at the bottom of the basket, attach the medium yo-yo to the block gathered side down, and the small yo-yo gathered side up. Add a button to the center.
3. Pink a strip, ½" x 42", for the basket bow; cut in half to make 2 strips. Place one end of each strip, right side down, under the basket; pin the remaining ends out of the way. Appliquilt the basket, catching the ends in the stitching. Tie the strips in a bow after you complete the quilt.

Block #2

Pink ½"-wide strips of green fabric for the stems. Make three-dimensional flowers (page 20) and attach them to the block with buttons or other embellishments. I placed a small doily in the center of each flower, under the button. A piece of lace or a circle of fabric would also work.

Block #3

1. Pink ⅜"-wide strips of green fabric for the stems.
2. Make yo-yos (page 19). For each flower, pin a doily or piece of lace or fabric to the block. (Use the yo-yo template (page 74) to pink circles of lace or fabric if you don't use doilies.) Center a yo-yo, gathered side down, on each doily and attach. On other doilies, attach silk roses or decorative buttons.

Block #4

1. Pink 2 strips of green fabric for the twining stems, one ⅜" x 29" and one ⅜" x 14". Tuck the ends under the basket at the points marked with an "X" on the basket template. Appliquilt the basket, catching the stem ends in the stitching.
2. Cut a 20" length of jute. Tie a knot at each end. Pink a strip of green fabric, ¼" x 18", for the handle stem. Twist the jute and stem together loosely; pin in place for the basket handle.
3. Make 20 buds (page 20). Attach the stems and basket handle to the block with the buds.

Block #5

Tuck 5 apples under the basket pieces, overlapping them; appliquilt in place. Appliquilt the last apple on top.

Block #6

1. Pink ¼"-wide strips of green fabric for the stems. Arrange the basket pieces on the block and tuck the stems under the top of the basket; appliquilt in place.
2. Make 16 three-dimensional flower petals (page 20).
3. Make 8 yo-yos (page 19). Attach the yo-yos to the block with the gathered side down.
4. Place a petal on each side of each yo-yo, overlapping the ends of the petals where they meet the stem. Tack the ends of the petals with square knots as shown.

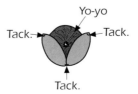

Yo-yo
Tack. Tack.
Tack.

Blocks #7, #8, and #9

You can stitch these blocks separately or join them before appliquilting. The three-block unit is still easy to work with, but it is not as portable as individual blocks.

1. Appliquilt the fence pieces, from left to right. If you have joined the blocks into a unit, you can cover the seams with the fence pieces.
2. Pink 2 strips, each ½" x 30", from different green fabrics for the stems.
3. Pink 2 sunflower pieces for each flower, using contrasting fabrics. Place one piece on top of the other so that all petals show. Place the flower center on top of petal pieces and appliquilt, leaving the petals free.
4. Make 22 three-dimensional daisy petals (page 20). Overlap the points at one end and attach each flower to the block with a button. Tack the petals at the outer tips with square knots.
5. Appliquilt the nail over the basket handle.
6. Make 3 yo-yo flowers (page 19). Attach them to the hanging basket with buttons.

Assembling and Finishing the Quilt

1. Arrange the blocks as shown in the block layout and quilt plan. Join the blocks into rows; join the rows (page 15).
2. Appliquilt the leaves over the seams, joining the blocks in the top 2 rows.
3. Fold the 1"-wide inner border strips in half lengthwise, wrong sides together, and press. With raw edges aligned and the fold toward the center, pin the strips to the edges.
4. Add the side borders; add the top and bottom borders (page 17). Once the borders are attached, ¼" of the inner border will show.
5. Using the leaf quilting template on page 72, randomly trace leaf shapes onto the outer border; connect the leaves with curved lines. Quilt the outer border in contrasting perle cotton.
6. Bind the edges using your favorite method or the appliquilt method (page 18).
7. Attach buttons as desired. Label your quilt.

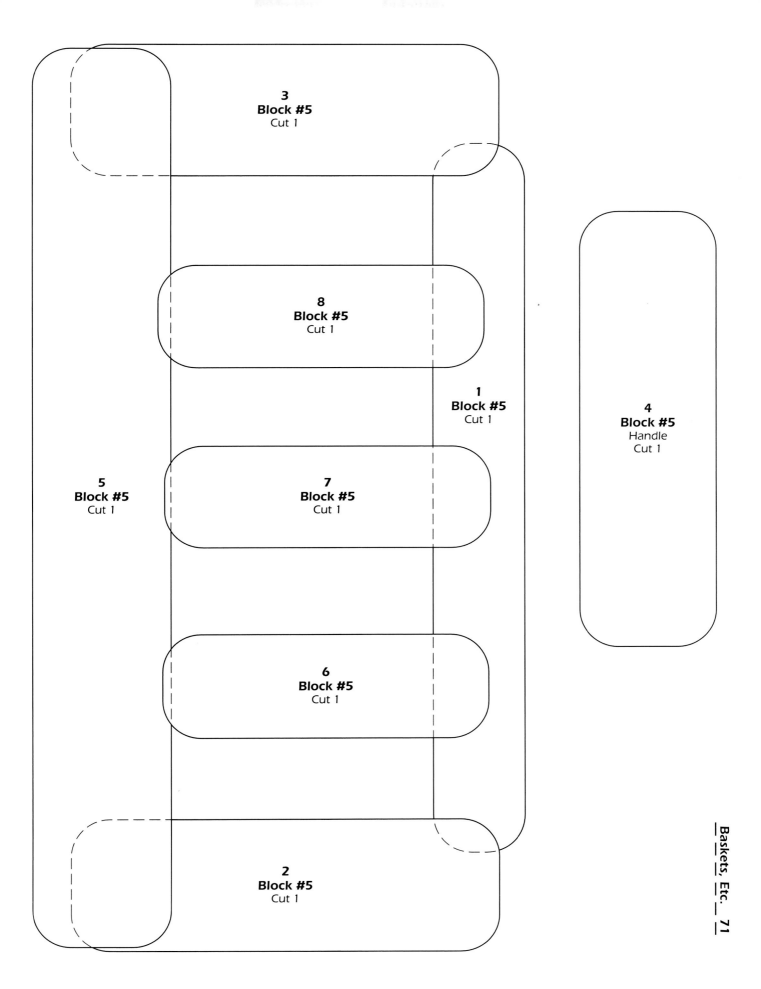

3
Block #5
Cut 1

8
Block #5
Cut 1

1
Block #5
Cut 1

4
Block #5
Handle
Cut 1

5
Block #5
Cut 1

7
Block #5
Cut 1

6
Block #5
Cut 1

2
Block #5
Cut 1

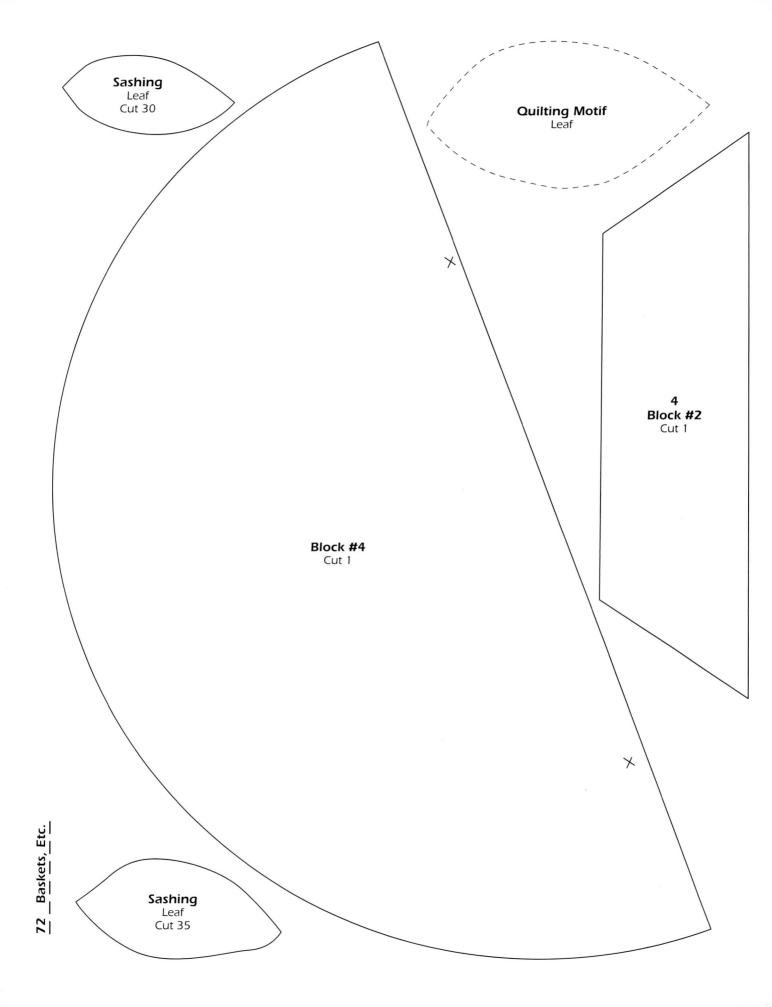

Sashing
Leaf
Cut 30

Quilting Motif
Leaf

4
Block #2
Cut 1

Block #4
Cut 1

Sashing
Leaf
Cut 35

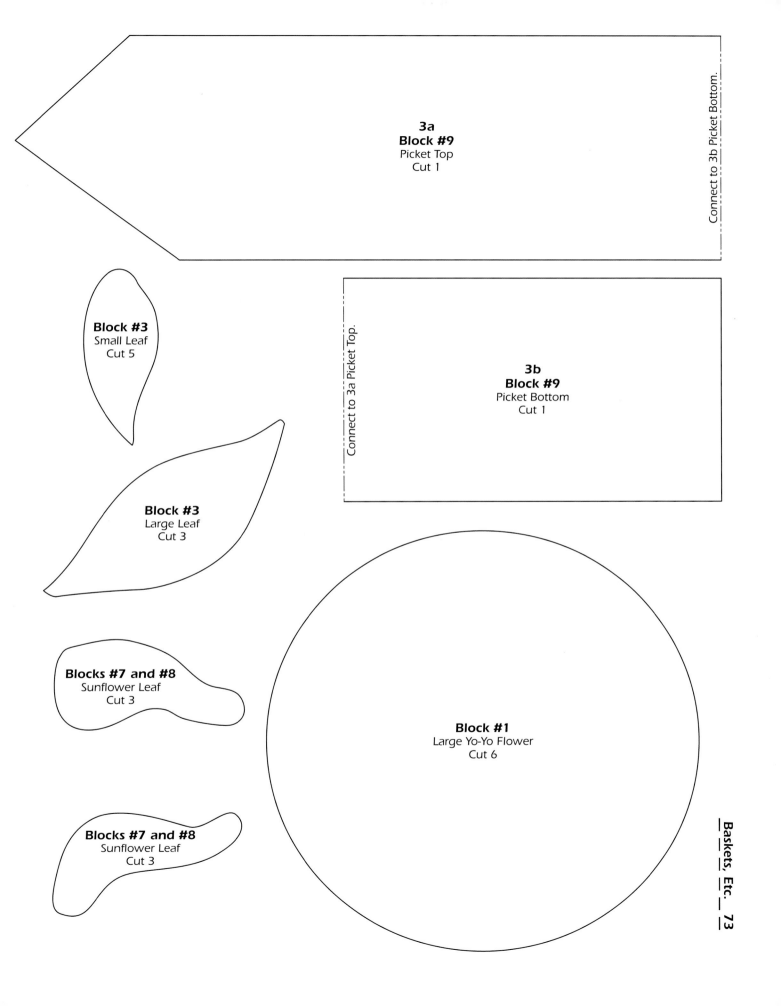

3a
Block #9
Picket Top
Cut 1

Connect to 3b Picket Bottom.

Block #3
Small Leaf
Cut 5

Connect to 3a Picket Top.

3b
Block #9
Picket Bottom
Cut 1

Block #3
Large Leaf
Cut 3

Blocks #7 and #8
Sunflower Leaf
Cut 3

Block #1
Large Yo-Yo Flower
Cut 6

Blocks #7 and #8
Sunflower Leaf
Cut 3

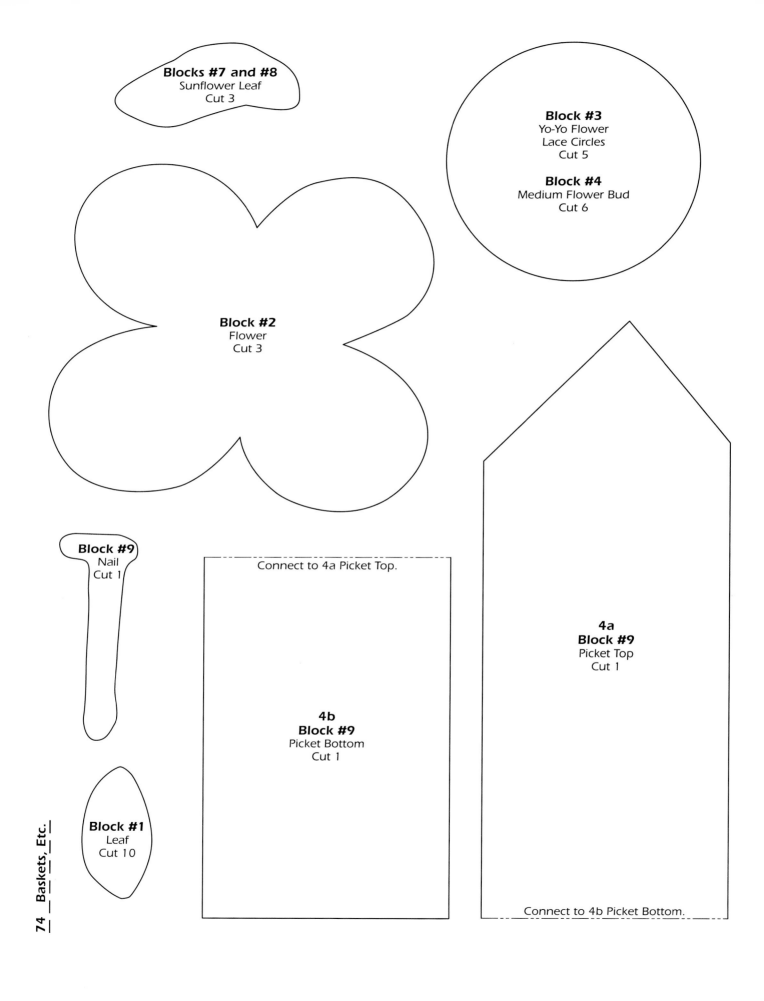

Blocks #7 and #8
Sunflower Leaf
Cut 3

Block #3
Yo-Yo Flower
Lace Circles
Cut 5

Block #4
Medium Flower Bud
Cut 6

Block #2
Flower
Cut 3

Block #9
Nail
Cut 1

Connect to 4a Picket Top.

4a
Block #9
Picket Top
Cut 1

4b
Block #9
Picket Bottom
Cut 1

Block #1
Leaf
Cut 10

Connect to 4b Picket Bottom.

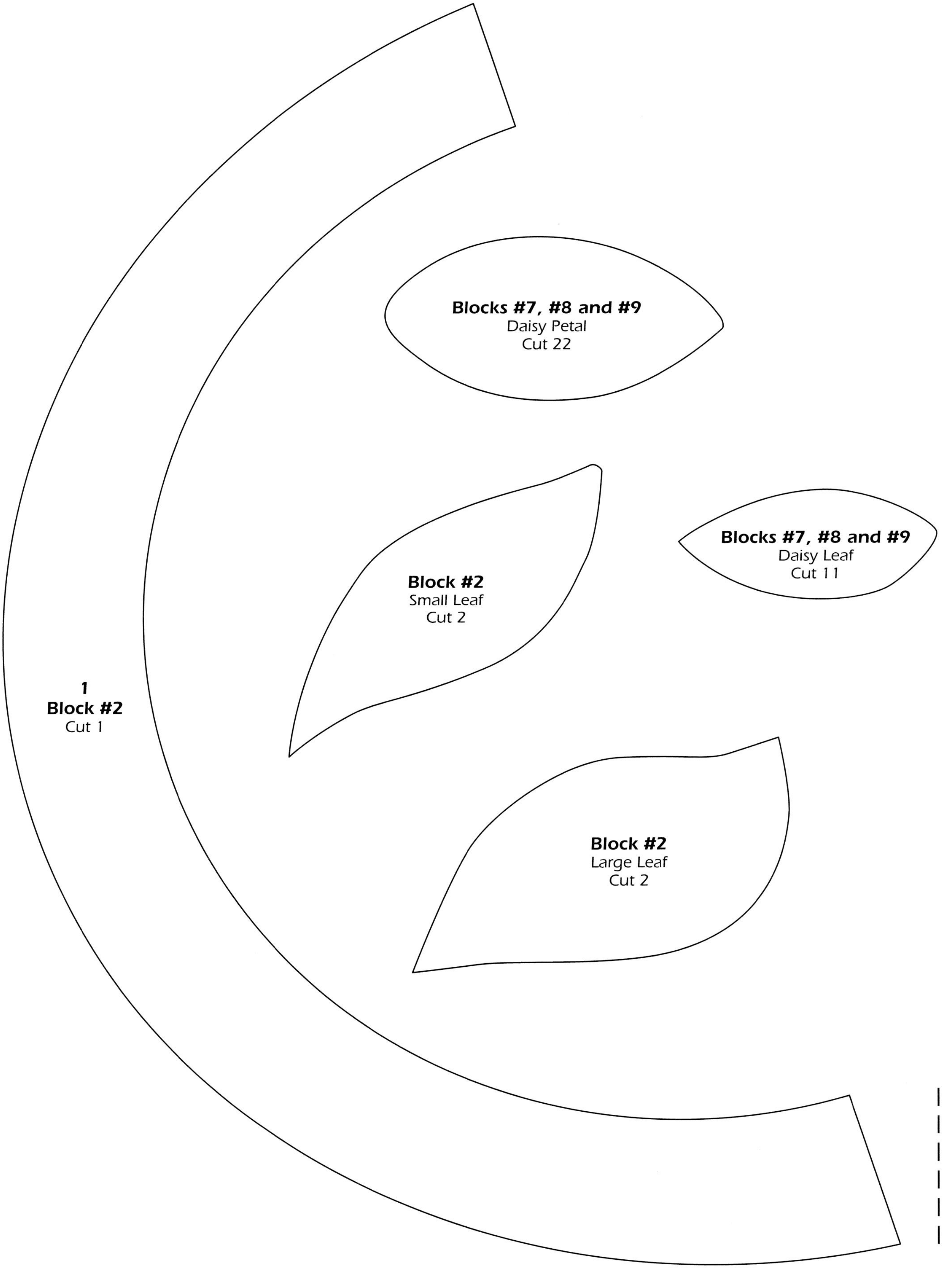

Blocks #7, #8 and #9
Daisy Petal
Cut 22

Blocks #7, #8 and #9
Daisy Leaf
Cut 11

Block #2
Small Leaf
Cut 2

1
Block #2
Cut 1

Block #2
Large Leaf
Cut 2

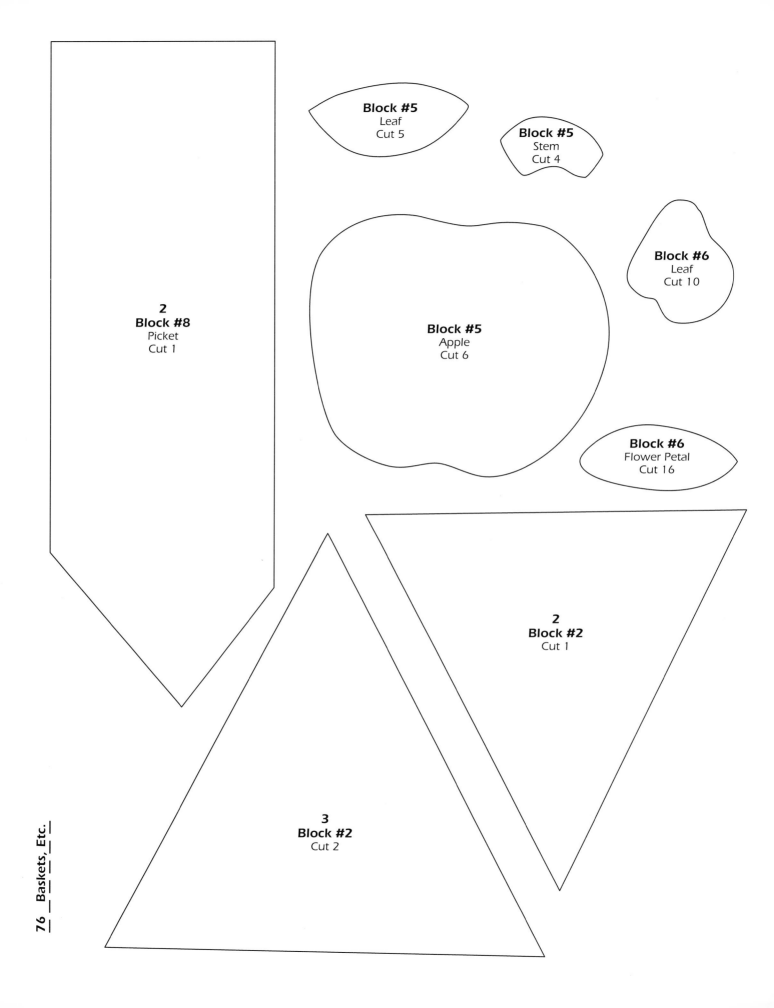

Block #5
Leaf
Cut 5

Block #5
Stem
Cut 4

Block #6
Leaf
Cut 10

2
Block #8
Picket
Cut 1

Block #5
Apple
Cut 6

Block #6
Flower Petal
Cut 16

2
Block #2
Cut 1

3
Block #2
Cut 2

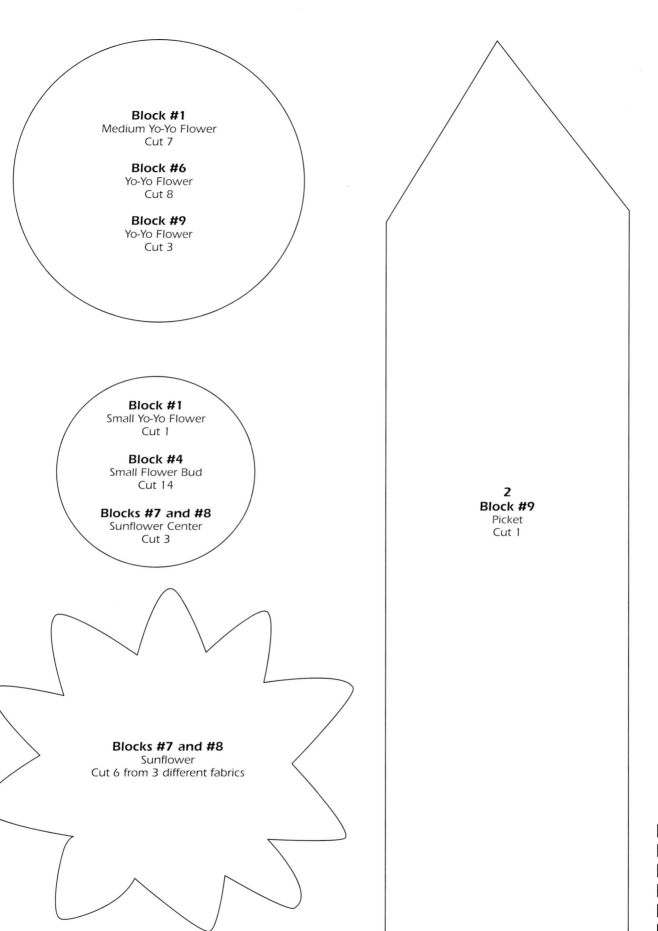

Block #1
Medium Yo-Yo Flower
Cut 7

Block #6
Yo-Yo Flower
Cut 8

Block #9
Yo-Yo Flower
Cut 3

Block #1
Small Yo-Yo Flower
Cut 1

Block #4
Small Flower Bud
Cut 14

Blocks #7 and #8
Sunflower Center
Cut 3

2
Block #9
Picket
Cut 1

Blocks #7 and #8
Sunflower
Cut 6 from 3 different fabrics

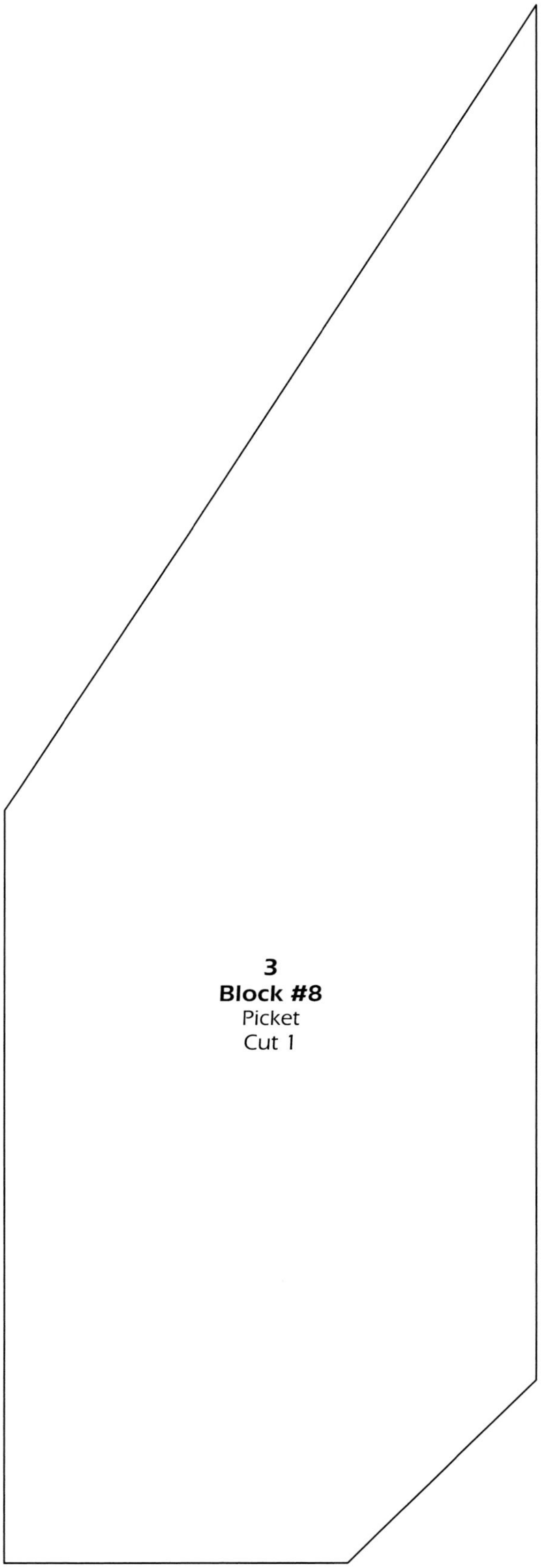

3
Block #8
Picket
Cut 1

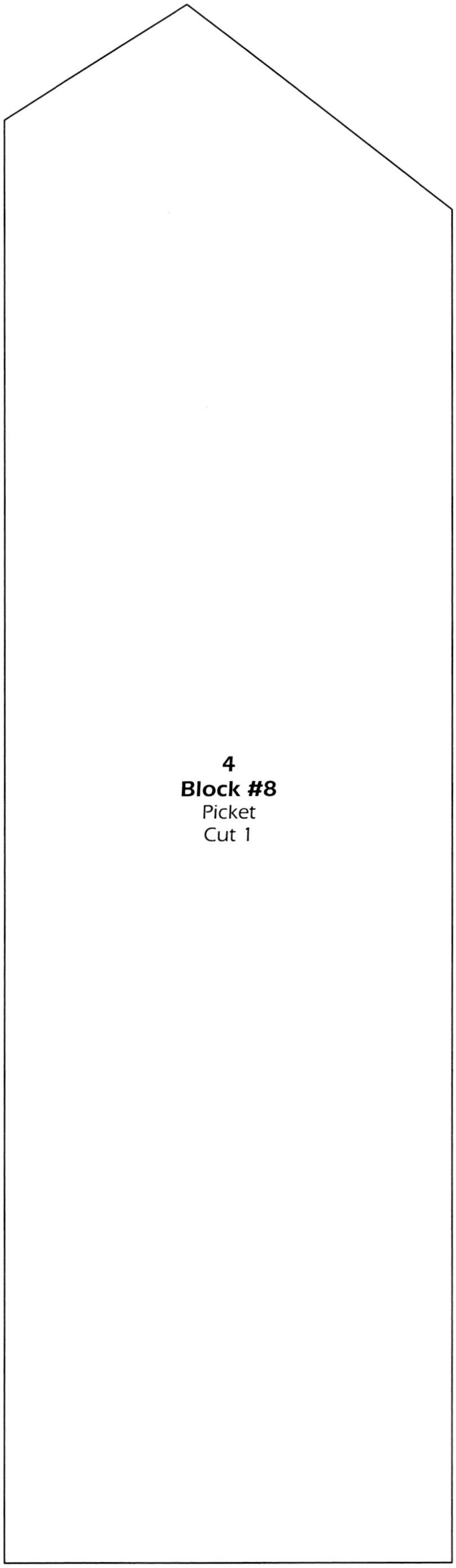

4
Block #8
Picket
Cut 1

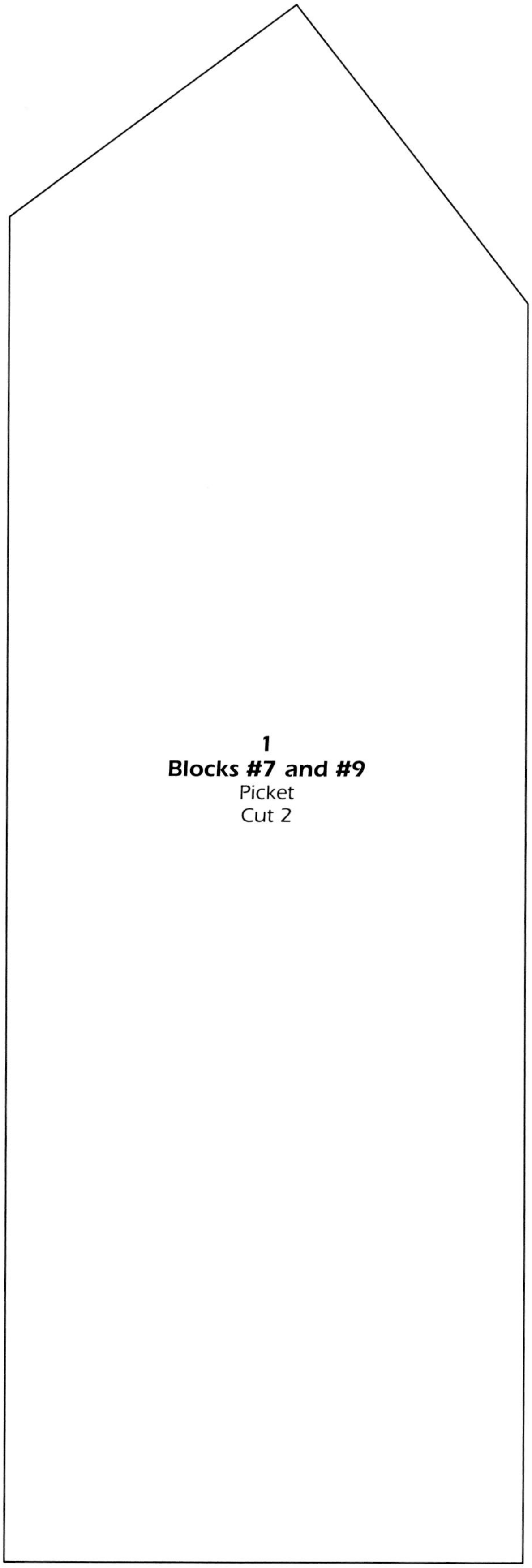

1
Blocks #7 and #9
Picket
Cut 2

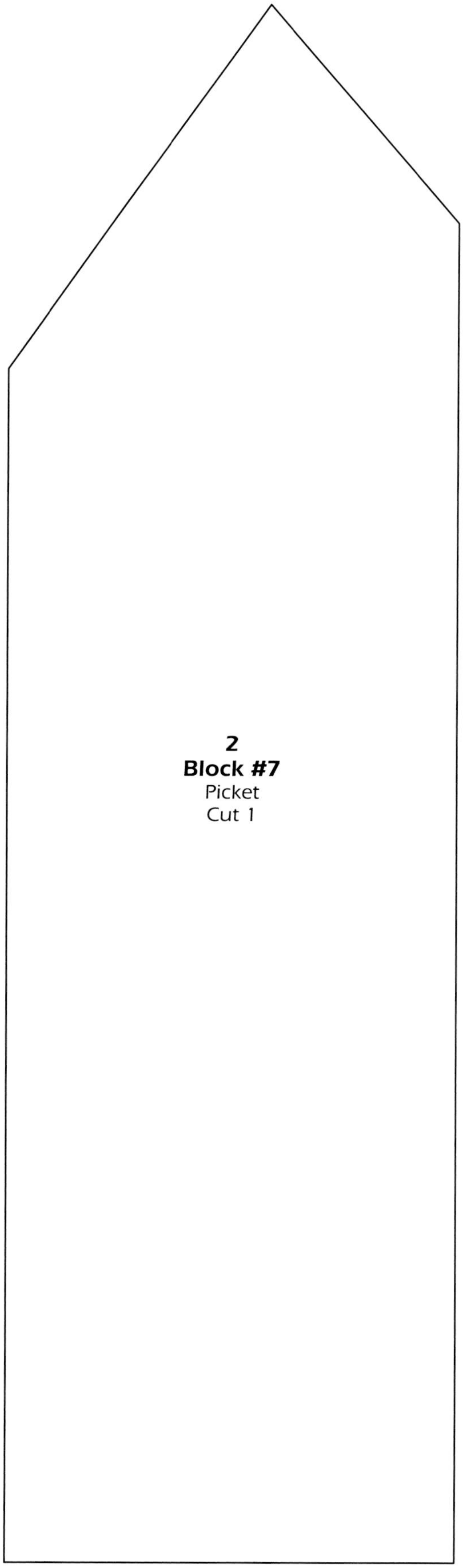

2
Block #7
Picket
Cut 1

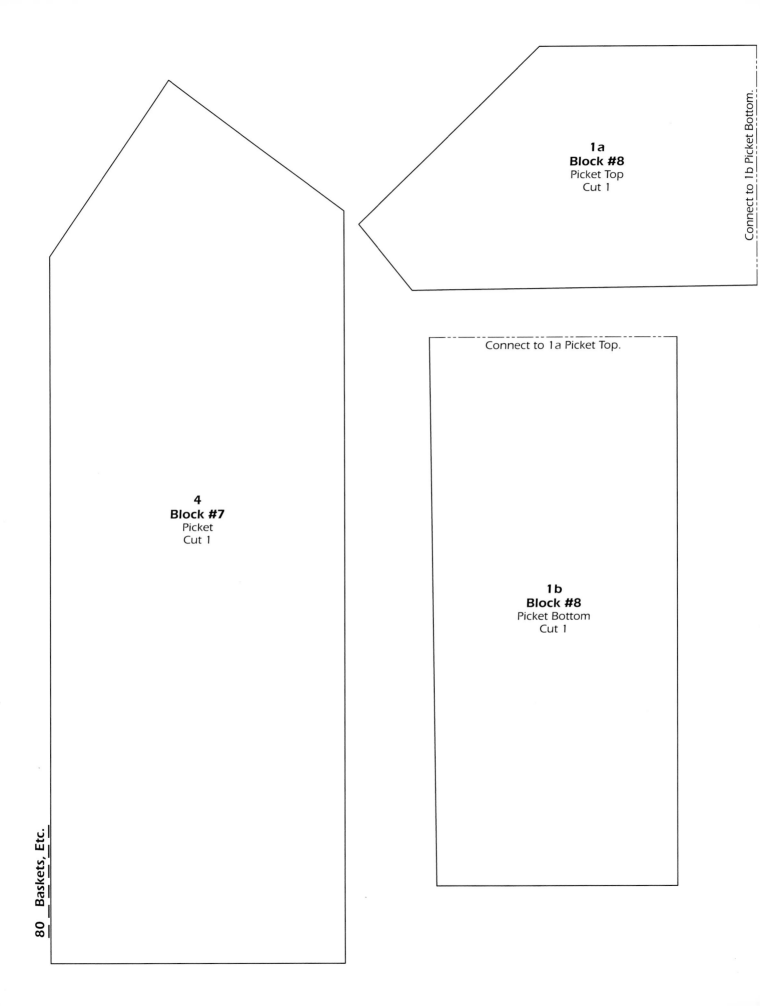

1a
Block #8
Picket Top
Cut 1

Connect to 1b Picket Bottom.

Connect to 1a Picket Top.

4
Block #7
Picket
Cut 1

1b
Block #8
Picket Bottom
Cut 1

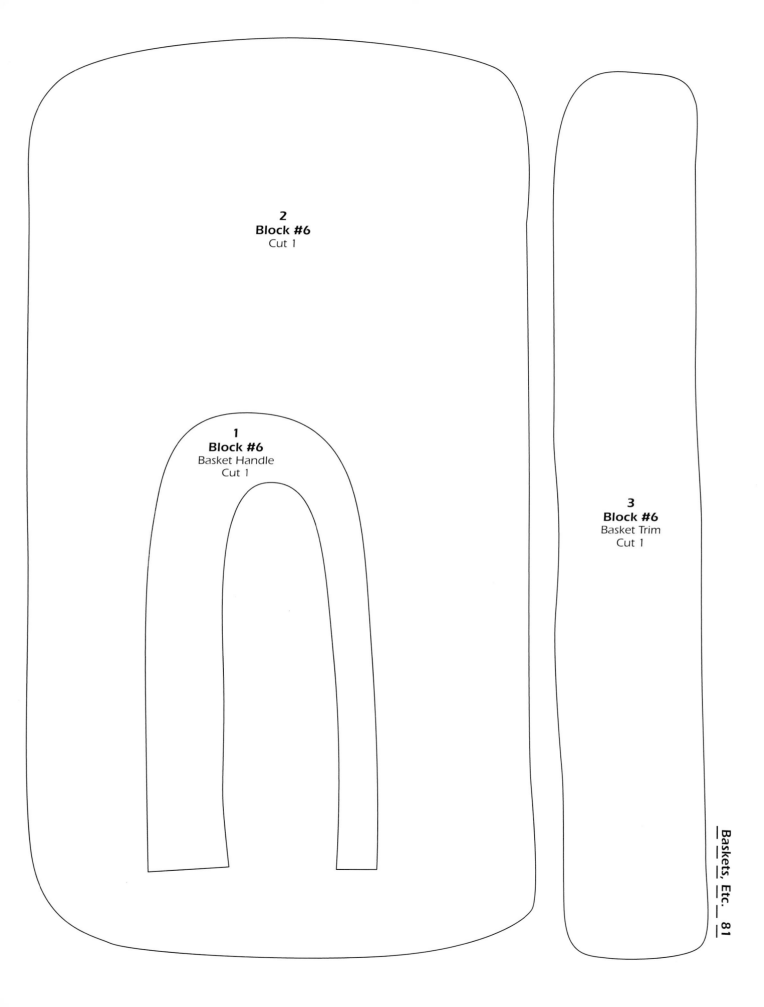

2
Block #6
Cut 1

1
Block #6
Basket Handle
Cut 1

3
Block #6
Basket Trim
Cut 1

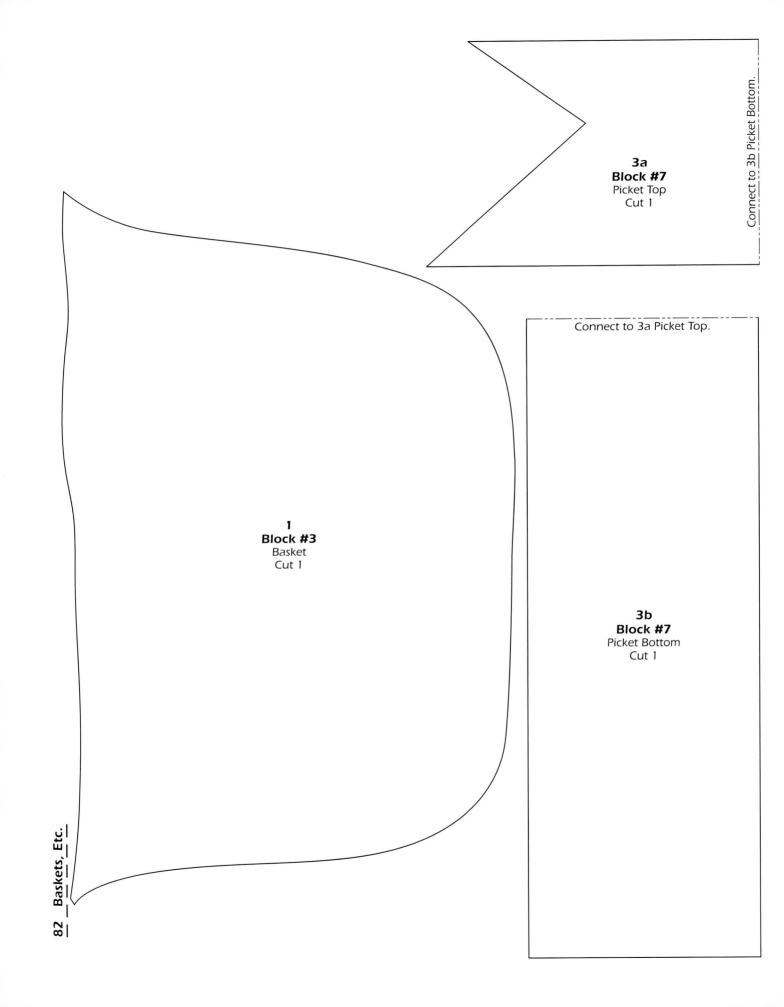

3a
Block #7
Picket Top
Cut 1

Connect to 3a Picket Top.

1
Block #3
Basket
Cut 1

3b
Block #7
Picket Bottom
Cut 1

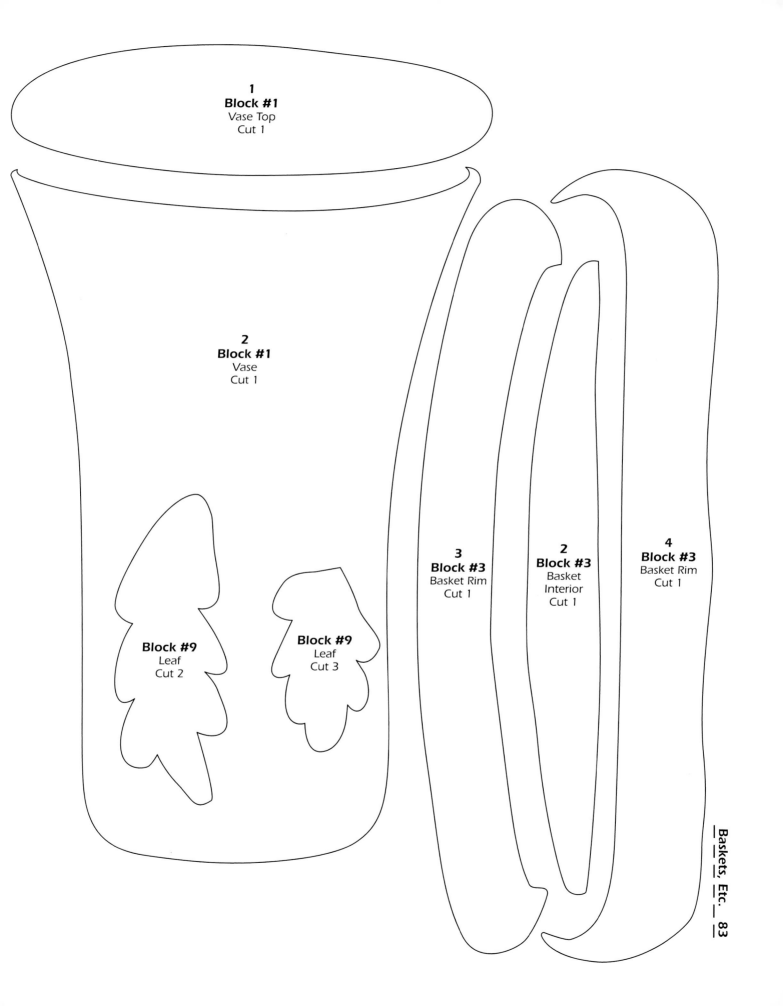

1
Block #1
Vase Top
Cut 1

2
Block #1
Vase
Cut 1

Block #9
Leaf
Cut 2

Block #9
Leaf
Cut 3

3
Block #3
Basket Rim
Cut 1

2
Block #3
*Basket
Interior*
Cut 1

4
Block #3
Basket Rim
Cut 1

Halloween Sampler

Plaids and stripes add a primitive flavor to traditional Halloween motifs.

Color photo: page 23
Size: 24" x 28"
Materials: 44"-wide fabric

1/3 yd. large-scale plaid for background

1/3 yd. black solid for background and binding

1/3 yd. small-scale plaid for background

Assorted scraps for appliqués and Log Cabin block

5/8 yd. Pellon fleece or other thin batting

3/4 yd. fabric for backing

1/4 yd. fabric for border

Perle cotton in orange and black

Embroidery floss in ecru and green

Stiff linen thread

Doll hair

Buttons of your choice

Embellishments of your choice, such as spider web

Cutting

Refer to the block layout below as you cut.

Block #1	Block #2	Block #3
Block #4	Block #5	Block #6

Block Layout Diagram

From the large-scale plaid, cut:
1 rectangle, 9" x 12¾", for block #2

From the black fabric, cut:
1 square, 8¾" x 8¾", for block #3
1 rectangle, 8¾" x 12¾", for block #4
1 rectangle, 8¾" x 9", for block #5

From the small-scale plaid, cut:
1 rectangle, 8¾" x 12¾", for block #6

From the assorted scraps, cut:
1 square, 2½" x 2½", for center of block #1
3 light strips, each 1½" wide, for block #1
3 dark strips, each 1½" wide, for block #1

From the batting, cut:
- 2 squares, each 10" x 10", for blocks #1 and #3
- 1 rectangle, 8" x 14", for block #2
- 2 rectangles, each 10" x 14", for blocks #4 and #6
- 1 rectangle, 8" x 10", for block #5

From the backing fabric, cut:
- 2 squares, each 10½" x 10½", for blocks #1 and #3
- 1 rectangle, 9" x 14½", for block #2
- 2 rectangles, each 10½" x 14½", for blocks #4 and #6
- 1 rectangle, 9" x 10½", for block #5

From the border fabric, cut:
- 2 strips, each 2½" x 20½", for side borders
- 2 strips, each 2½" x 28", for top and bottom borders

Making the Log Cabin Block

Using the 2½" square and 1½" strips you cut from scraps, make the Log Cabin block #1.

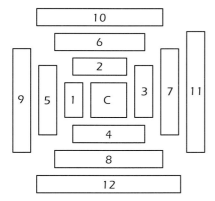

Making the Block Sandwiches

Refer to the instructions on pages 10–12 to layer and label the block sandwiches.

Appliquilting the Blocks

Use the templates on pages 86–87 and on the pullout pattern. Refer to the quilt plan for layout of the pieces. The numbers on the templates indicate the stitching order.

1. Make the templates and cut out the appliqué pieces, referring to the instructions on page 13.
2. Appliquilt the pieces, referring to the instructions on page 14. Special instructions for specific blocks follow.

Block #2: Witch

1. Appliquilt the witch's face. Attach the doll hair to each side of the head; appliquilt the hat, brim, and band over the hair.
2. For the witch's dress, cut a 5" x 5" square. For the cape, cut a 3" x 5" rectangle.
3. Knot a 12" length of perle cotton or embroidery floss and gather the top of the dress. Position the dress with the gathers at the neck and sew in place. Repeat with the cape.
4. Tack the lower corners of the dress and cape to the block with square knots.

Block #3: Cat

Sew 4½" loops of stiff linen thread to the cat for whiskers; clip the loops.

Block #4: House

Do not appliquilt the roof until the borders are added. Using 2 strands of ecru embroidery floss, backstitch (page 20) the fence and smoke.

Block #5: Pumpkin

Using 2 strands of green embroidery floss, backstitch the pumpkin tendril.

Block #6: Ghost

Stitch the patch to the ghost with straight stitches.

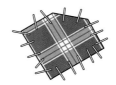

Assembling and Finishing the Quilt

1. Arrange the blocks as shown in the block layout and quilt plan.
2. Join the blocks in the following order, using the technique described on page 15: Sew block #1 to block #4, block #2 to block #5, and block #3 to block #6. Join the units.
3. Cross-stitch (page 16) the seams if desired.
4. Add the top and bottom borders; add the side borders (page 17).
5. Appliquilt the roof to the house and border.
6. Bind the edges using your favorite method or the appliquilt method (page 18).
7. Attach buttons as desired. Label your quilt.

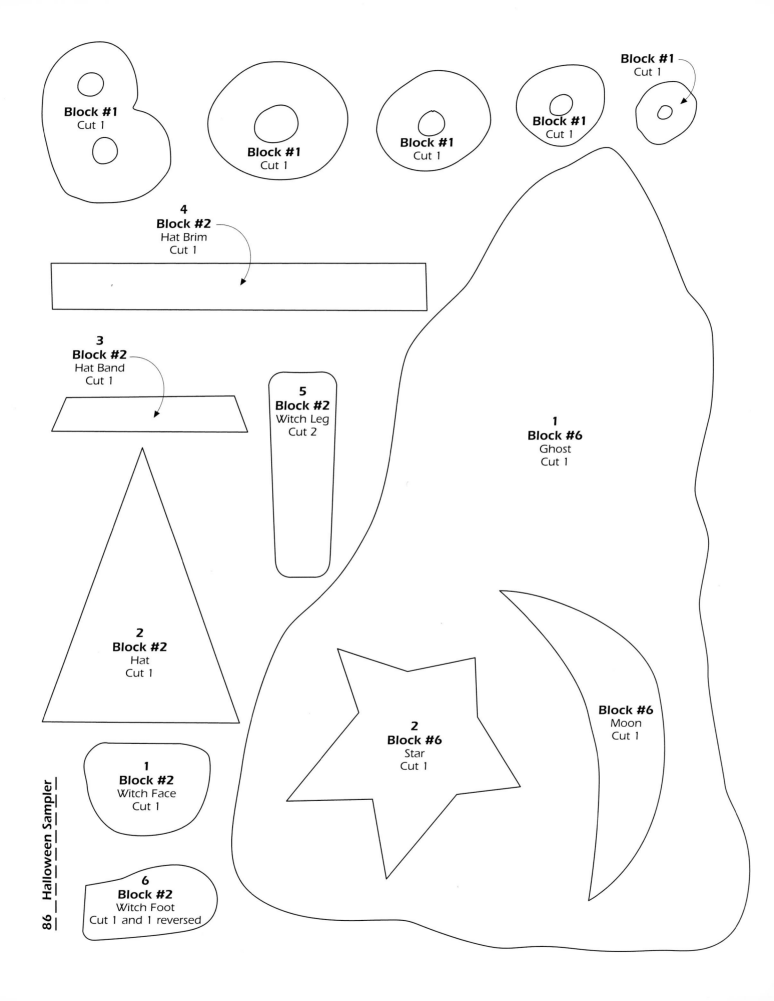

Block #1
Cut 1

Block #1
Cut 1

Block #1
Cut 1

Block #1
Cut 1

Block #1
Cut 1

4
Block #2
Hat Brim
Cut 1

3
Block #2
Hat Band
Cut 1

5
Block #2
Witch Leg
Cut 2

1
Block #6
Ghost
Cut 1

2
Block #2
Hat
Cut 1

1
Block #2
Witch Face
Cut 1

2
Block #6
Star
Cut 1

Block #6
Moon
Cut 1

6
Block #2
Witch Foot
Cut 1 and 1 reversed

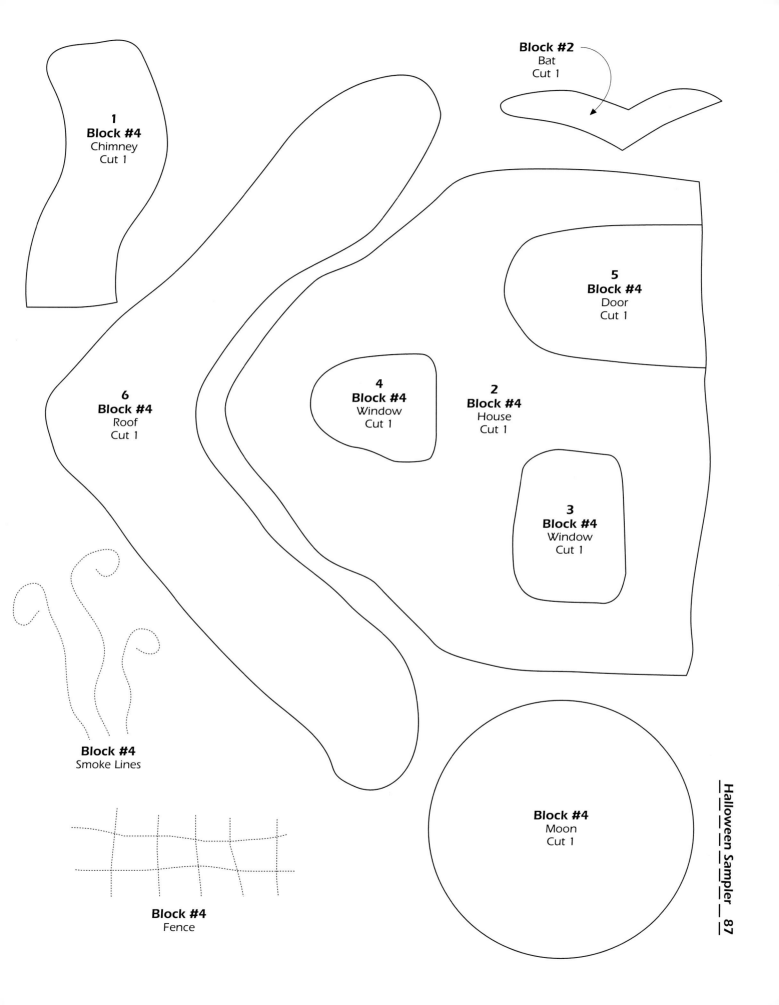

1
Block #4
Chimney
Cut 1

Block #2
Bat
Cut 1

5
Block #4
Door
Cut 1

6
Block #4
Roof
Cut 1

4
Block #4
Window
Cut 1

2
Block #4
House
Cut 1

3
Block #4
Window
Cut 1

Block #4
Smoke Lines

Block #4
Moon
Cut 1

Block #4
Fence

Nantucket

Anyone who loves the sea will enjoy this nautical wall hanging. Personalize it by including a map of your favorite island.

Color photo: page 21
Size: 32" x 26"
Materials: 44"-wide fabric

Background Fabrics
   ⅜ yd. star print for lighthouse and boat
   Assorted scraps for appliqué pieces
¾ yd. Pellon fleece or other thin batting
1 yd. fabric for backing
¼ yd. plaid fabric for side and top borders
¼ yd. light fabric for bottom border
Assorted scraps for the appliqué pieces
¼ yd. fabric for binding
Perle cotton in assorted colors
Jute
Buttons of your choice

Cutting

Refer to the block layout below as you cut.

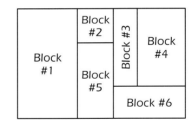

Block Layout Diagram

From the background fabrics, cut:
   1 rectangle, 10¾" x 20½", for Lighthouse block
   1 rectangle, 7" x 6¾", for Star block
   1 rectangle, 5" x 14¾", for Fish block
   1 rectangle, 8¾" x 14¾", for Boat block
   1 rectangle, 7" x 14¾", for Bird block
   1 rectangle, 6¾" x 12¾", for Map block

From the batting, cut:
- 1 rectangle, 12" x 26", for Lighthouse block
- 1 rectangle, 6" x 8", for Star block
- 1 rectangle, 6" x 18", for Bird block
- 1 rectangle, 4" x 16", for Fish block
- 1 rectangle, 10" x 16", for Boat block
- 1 rectangle, 10" x 14", for Map block

From the backing fabric, cut:
- 1 rectangle, 12½" x 26", for Lighthouse block
- 1 rectangle, 7" x 8½", for Star block
- 1 rectangle, 7" x 18½", for Bird block
- 1 rectangle, 5" x 16½", for Fish block
- 1 rectangle, 10½" x 16½", for Boat block
- 1 rectangle, 10½" x 14½", for Map block

From the plaid border fabric, cut:
- 1 strip, 2½" x 28½", for top border
- 2 strips, each 2½" x 26", for side borders

From the light fabric, cut:
- 1 strip, 4½" x 28½", for bottom border

Making the Block Sandwiches

Refer to the instructions on pages 10–12 to layer and label the block sandwiches.

Appliquilting the Blocks

Use the templates on pages 90–93 and the pull-out pattern. Refer to the quilt plan for layout of the pieces. The numbers on the templates indicate the stitching order.

1. Make the templates and cut out the appliqué pieces, referring to the instructions on page 13. You may vary the size and shape of the lighthouse base, as long as the piece covers the lower edges of the lighthouse. The same is true of the wave in the bird block.
2. Appliquilt the pieces, referring to the instructions on page 14. Special instructions for specific blocks follow.

Block #1: Lighthouse

If you use a print with a rock design for the lighthouse base, you may want to appliquilt interior lines for added dimension.

Block #2: Star

Overlap the star pieces carefully to prevent the background from showing.

Block #4: Boat

Do not appliquilt the boat railing until the blocks and borders are joined.

Block #5: Bird

1. Arrange the pieces; then appliquilt the pieces in place, except for shorebird #1. Appliquilt the shorebird after the blocks are joined.
2. Embroider the seagulls and bird legs using 2 strands of embroidery floss and a backstitch (page 20).

Block #6: Map

Transfer the words and details using a transfer pen, following the manufacturer's instructions carefully. Using 2 strands of embroidery floss, backstitch the words and the details.

Assembling and Finishing the Quilt

1. Arrange the blocks as shown in the block layout and quilt plan.
2. Join the blocks (page 15) in the following order: Sew block #2 to block #3; sew this unit to block #1. Sew block #4 to block #5; sew this unit to block #6. Join the units.
3. Fly-stitch (page 16) the seams if desired.
4. Add the top and bottom borders; add the side borders (page 17).
5. Appliquilt the whales to the bottom border.
6. Appliquilt shorebird #1 and the boat railing, overlapping the seams
7. Bind the edges using your favorite method or the appliquilt method (page 18).
8. Machine stitch 2 short pieces of jute to the fish; tack the ends to the border with a button.
9. Attach buttons as desired. Label your quilt.

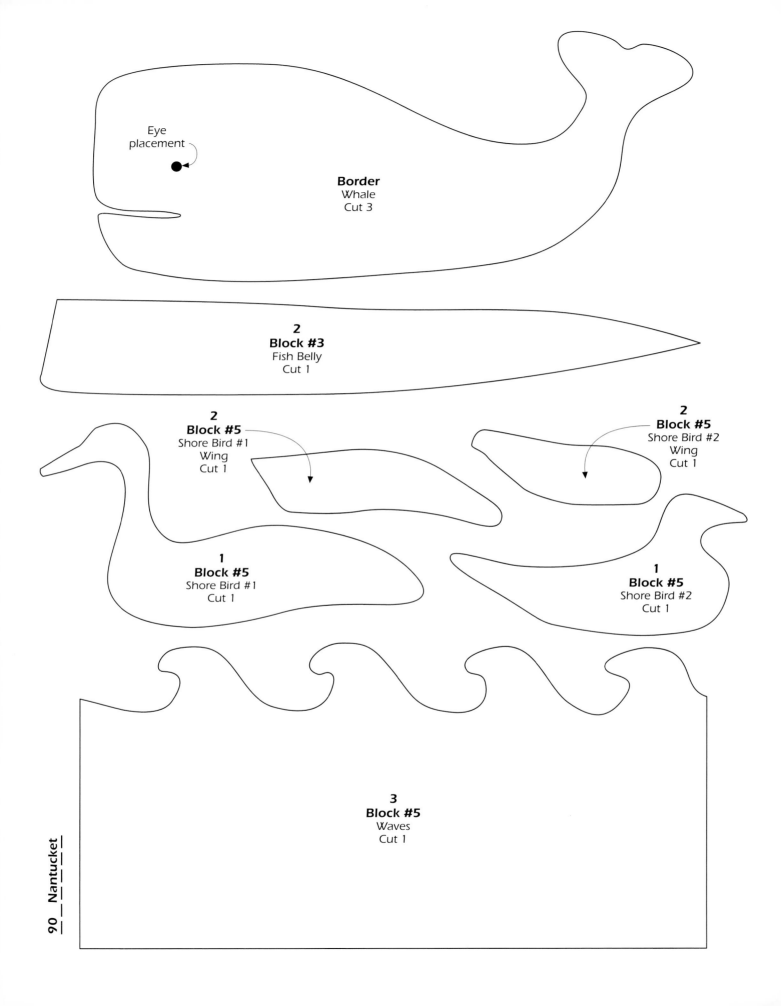

Eye placement

Border
Whale
Cut 3

2
Block #3
Fish Belly
Cut 1

2
Block #5
Shore Bird #1
Wing
Cut 1

2
Block #5
Shore Bird #2
Wing
Cut 1

1
Block #5
Shore Bird #1
Cut 1

1
Block #5
Shore Bird #2
Cut 1

3
Block #5
Waves
Cut 1

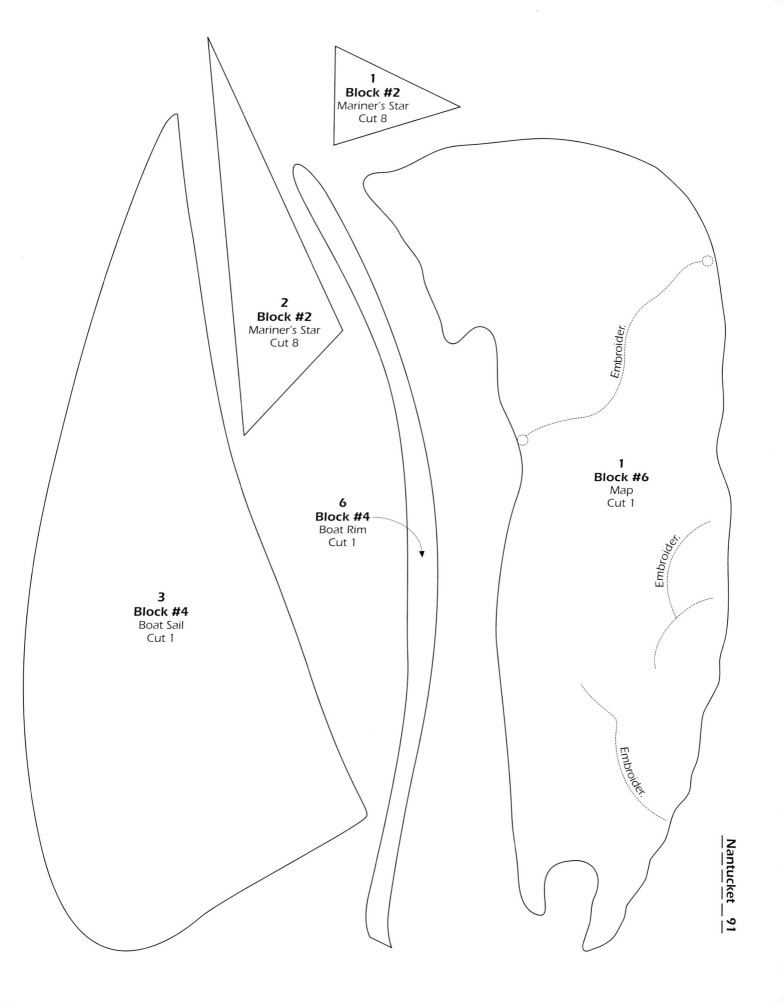

1
Block #2
Mariner's Star
Cut 8

2
Block #2
Mariner's Star
Cut 8

6
Block #4
Boat Rim
Cut 1

3
Block #4
Boat Sail
Cut 1

1
Block #6
Map
Cut 1

Embroider.

Embroider.

Embroider.

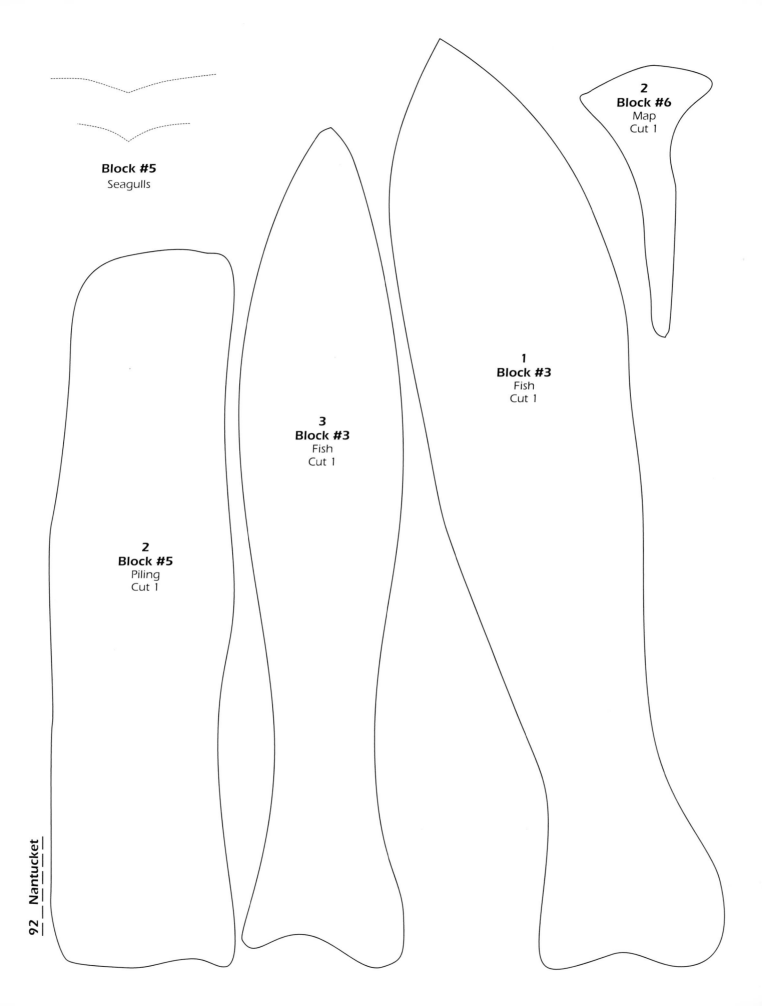

Block #5
Seagulls

2
Block #6
Map
Cut 1

2
Block #5
Piling
Cut 1

3
Block #3
Fish
Cut 1

1
Block #3
Fish
Cut 1

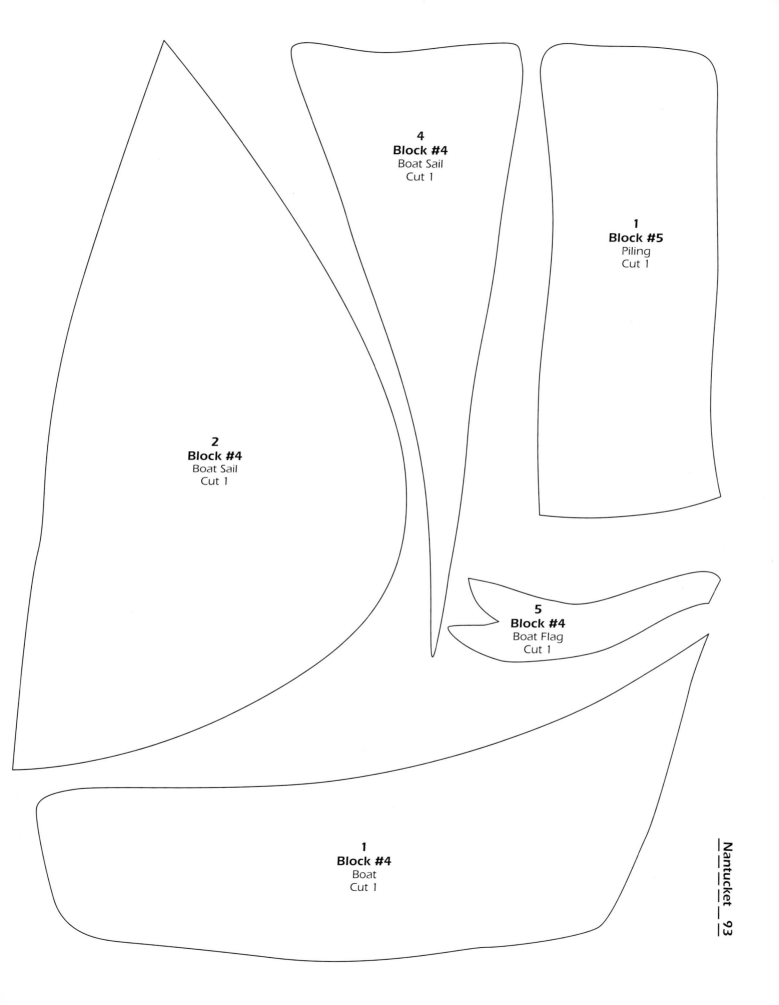

4
Block #4
Boat Sail
Cut 1

1
Block #5
Piling
Cut 1

2
Block #4
Boat Sail
Cut 1

5
Block #4
Boat Flag
Cut 1

1
Block #4
Boat
Cut 1

Americana

Show your patriotism when you display this folk-art wall hanging. Bring it out for Independence Day, or hang it year 'round.

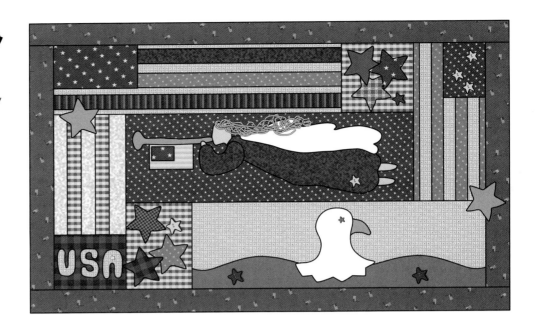

Color photo: page 21
40" x 25"
Materials: 44"-wide fabric

Background Fabrics

¼ yd. print for eagle

¼ yd. print for angel

¼ yd. each of light, medium, and dark prints for flags

¼ yd. plaid for star

¾ yd. Pellon fleece or other thin batting

1⅛ yds. fabric for backing

⅜ yd. fabric for borders

Assorted scraps for appliqué pieces

¼ yd. fabric for binding

Perle cotton in assorted colors

Yellow yarn for angel hair

Buttons of your choice

Embellishments of your choice

Fabric stiffener

Cutting

Refer to the block layout below as you cut.

Block #1	Block #2	Block #3
Block #4 / Block #6	Block #5	
	Block #7	

Block Layout Diagram

From the background fabrics, cut:

1 rectangle, 6¾" x 24¾", for upper Flag block

1 rectangle, 8" x 25", for Angel block

1 rectangle, 8¾" x 24¾", for Eagle block

1 rectangle, 6¾" x 15¾", for left Flag block

1 rectangle, 7" x 8¾", for lower Star block

1 rectangle, 6¾" x 7", for upper Star block

1 rectangle, 6¾" x 13¾", for right Flag block

From the batting, cut:

1 rectangle, 8" x 26", for upper Flag block

1 rectangle, 7" x 24", for Angel block

1 rectangle, 10" x 26", for Eagle block

1 rectangle, 8" x 17", for left Flag block

1 rectangle, 6" x 10", for lower Star block

1 rectangle, 6" x 8", for upper Star block

1 rectangle, 8" x 15", for right Flag block

From the backing fabrics, cut:
- 1 rectangle, 8½" x 26½", for upper Flag block
- 1 rectangle, 8" x 25", for Angel block
- 1 rectangle, 10½" x 26½", for Eagle block
- 1 rectangle, 8½" x 17½", for left Flag block
- 1 rectangle, 7" x 10½", for lower Star block
- 1 rectangle, 7" x 8½", for upper Star block
- 1 rectangle, 8½" x 15½", for right Flag block

From the border fabric, cut:
- 2 strips, each 2½" x 36½", for top and bottom borders
- 2 strips, each 2½" x 25½", for side borders

Making the Block Sandwiches

Refer to the instructions on pages 10–12 to layer and label the block sandwiches.

Appliquilting the Blocks

Use the templates on page 96 and the pullout pattern. Refer to the quilt plan for layout of the pieces. The numbers on the templates indicate the stitching order.

1. Make the templates and cut out the appliqué pieces, referring to the instructions on page 13.
2. Appliquilt the pieces, referring to the instructions on page 14. Special instructions for specific blocks follow.

Block #1: Upper Flag

Pink a 3¾" x 7" navy blue star rectangle. Pink two red strips, each 1¼" x 18", and one red strip, 1¼" x 24¾", for the flag stripes. (These measurements include seam allowances.) Appliquilt in place.

Block #3: Right Flag

Pink a 3½" x 4¾" navy blue star rectangle, two 1" x 9" light strips, and one 1" x 14" light strip for the flag stripes. Appliquilt in place.

Block #4: Left Flag

Pink a 4¾" x 6¾" navy blue rectangle for the USA background and two 1" x 11" light strips for the flag stripes. Appliquilt in place.

Block #5: Angel

1. To make the angel flag, cut a 2" x 3½" rectangle from backing fabric, fleece, and a scrap of red striped fabric. Appliquilt together at the edges. Cut a 1" x 1¾" rectangle of navy blue star fabric and appliquilt it to the upper left corner. Stiffen the flag with fabric stiffener. Sew lengths of perle cotton to the upper corners of the flag; tack the flag to the angel's horn.
2. Cut six 10" strands of yellow yarn. Fold the strands in half and attach them to the top of the angel's head. Using matching thread, tack the yarn in several places.

Block #7: Eagle

Appliquilt the wing, leaving the bottom edge free.

Assembling and Finishing the Quilt

1. Arrange the blocks as shown below.
2. Join the blocks in the following order, using the technique described on page 15: Sew blocks #1, #2, and #3 together to make Unit A. Sew blocks #5, #6, and #7 together, leaving 1½" of the lower left corner of the eagle wing free. Sew block #4 to the left edge of blocks #5, #6, and #7 to make Unit B. Join the units.

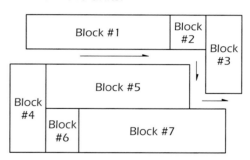

3. Cross-stitch (page 16) the seams if desired.
4. Add the top border. Add the bottom border, folding back the lower edge of the eagle wing. Add the right and left borders.
5. Appliquilt the gold stars over the seams.
6. Bind the edges with your favorite method or the appliquilt method (page 18).
7. Attach buttons as desired. Label your quilt.

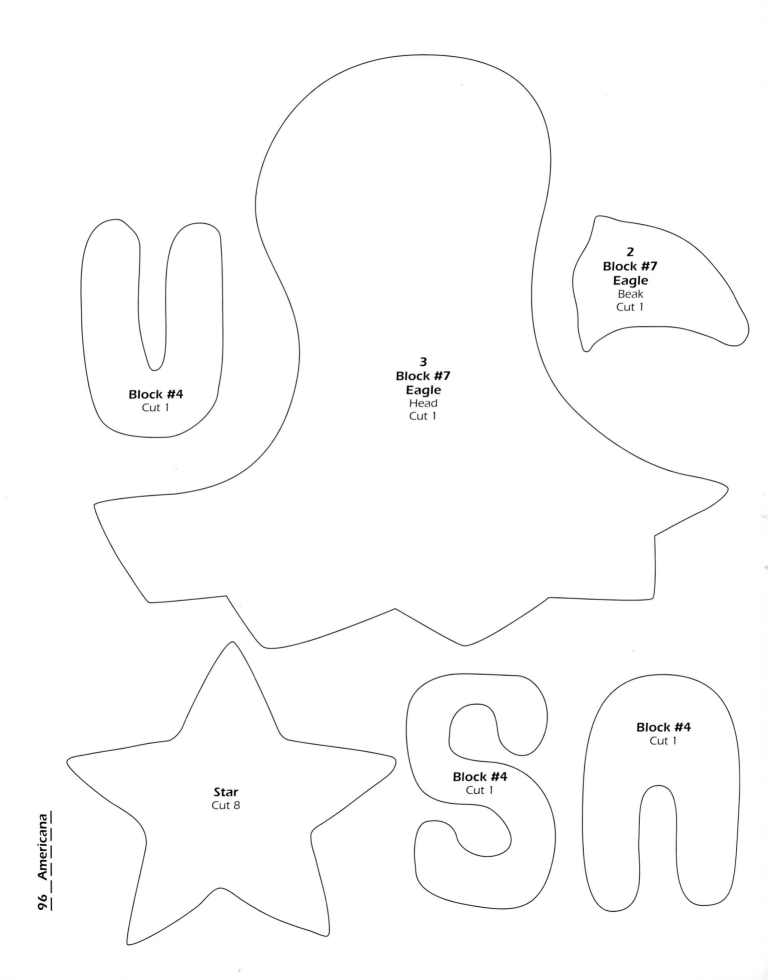

Block #4
Cut 1

2
Block #7
Eagle
Beak
Cut 1

3
Block #7
Eagle
Head
Cut 1

Star
Cut 8

Block #4
Cut 1

Block #4
Cut 1